D1736452

WHEN THE 49ERS WERE KINGS

HOW BILL WALSH AND
ED DeBARTOLO Jr. BUILT A FOOTBALL
DYNASTY IN SAN FRANCISCO

GORDON FORBES

SPORTS
PUBLISHING

Sports Publishing books may be purchased in bulk at special discounts for sales promotion, corporate gifts, fund-raising, or educational purposes. Special editions can also be created to specifications. For details, contact the Special Sales Department, Sports Publishing, 307 West 36th Street, 11th Floor, New York, NY 10018 or sportspubbooks@skyhorsepublishing.com.

Sports Publishing® is a registered trademark of Skyhorse Publishing, Inc.®, a Delaware corporation.

Visit our website at www.sportspubbooks.com.

10 9 8 7 6 5 4 3 2 1

Library of Congress Cataloging-in-Publication Data is available on file.

Interior photos by Associated Press

Cover design by Tom Lau
Cover photo credit: Associated Press

ISBN: 978-1-68358-249-6
Ebook ISBN: 978-1-68358-251-9

Printed in the United States of America

DEDICATION

THIS BOOK IS dedicated to three people, each linked to the San Francisco 49ers in different ways.

Edward DeBartolo Sr., who purchased the 49ers for his son in 1977 and inspired him to turn a unique football organization into a family.

Dwight Clark, the clutch receiver, who was drafted on the tenth round in 1979, but became a Pro Bowl star and made "The Catch" that propelled the 49ers to their first Super Bowl.

Geri Walsh, the wife of Hall of Fame Coach Bill Walsh, who suffered two strokes in 1999, but continued to engage in team activities and refrained from complaining about her husband's 80-hour work weeks.

TABLE OF CONTENTS

INTRODUCTION

SAN FRANCISCO HAS always been a city of extremes. The historic gold rush of 1849, followed by two major earthquakes in 1906 and 1989. Yuppies and hippies. The high-tech boom and bust of the 1990s. The island of Alcatraz, which opened as a cold, isolated prison in 1934, closed in 1963, and later emerged as a magnet for tourists.

More recently, a documentary entitled *California Typewriter* appeared in theatres. It proclaimed a renewed love affair among owners of aging Smith-Coronas who had divorced themselves from the Internet. One of the typewriter buffs featured Tom Hanks, the popular actor. Many of the scenes were filmed at a San Francisco store that gave the movie its name.

Aside from its unpredictable history, San Francisco has always been a special city, one made for dreamers and built on steep hills over which rattling cable cars climb halfway to the stars, as the song goes.

And on those chilly early mornings, when the sun sparkles through the ever-present mist, the City by the Bay becomes a magical place unlike any other in the world.

In 1979, as the city thinkers and artists tried to spread peace and love, San Francisco was rocked by a tragedy, a different kind of earthquake.

Two of its leaders, Mayor George Moscone and Harvey Milk, the city's first openly gay supervisor, were murdered by a disgruntled former employee.

Josh Getlin, a speechwriter for Moscone, gave the *Los Angeles Times* a first-hand account on the thirtieth anniversary of the murders:

> *A former supervisor, George White, suddenly appeared in the hall near my desk," recalled Getlin. "He walked to the mayor's office, two doors down. White shot the mayor four times, twice in the head.*

Getlin said White reloaded his .38-caliber revolver and shot Milk five times, then fled the building. He later surrendered to police.

Moscone, described by Getlin as a "sunny compassionate man," was a progressive mayor who campaigned on a platform of inclusion. He opened City Hall to gays, blacks, women, Latinos, Asians, and liberal thinkers. Following the murders, Dianne Feinstein, then a moderate, became the new mayor.

"The city was in deep despair," Feinstein was later to say at a press conference. Indeed, the city of dreams and disaster needed some kind of emotional lift. It was autumn, with a chill in the air and the bay glistening from the rays of the sun over a city saddened by the equivalent of a human earthquake.

* * *

Sports teams often offer some relief from the drudgery of real life. Yet, if there was any lingering emotion linked to the 49ers, the city's struggling pro football team, it would be hard to find. The 49ers were owned by sportsman Tony Morabito and his younger brother, Victor. Tony Morabito's attempt to secure a National Football League franchise had failed on two occasions, but he was able to join the new All-America Football Conference in 1946. The team played four seasons in the All-America Conference before it folded in 1949. Tony Morabito and three partners, including Victor, secured a National Football League franchise the next year, becoming the first major professional sports team in Northern California.

The first NFL 49ers were coached by Buck Shaw, an offensive genius. He believed that teams won by scoring touchdowns, not preventing them. Shaw brought in Y. A. Tittle, Joe Perry, John Henry Johnson, and Hugh McElhenny, forming a unique unit that came to be known as the "Million Dollar Backfield." All four were elected to the Pro Football Hall of Fame.

The 49ers' star-studded offense gave the fans who jammed aging Kezar Stadium plenty of big plays, once scoring 44 points on the NFL champion Los Angeles Rams. Yet, over a 27-year period, the 49ers never won a league championship and made the playoffs only twice. When the Morabito brothers both died of heart attacks (Tony Morabito collapsed and died while watching a game against the Chicago Bears in 1957, while Victor passed in 1964), their heirs eventually decided to divorce themselves from football and those frustrating afternoons at Kezar.

The Kezar guest box where Morabito suffered his fatal heart attack was located adjacent to the press box. Many an East Coast sportswriter covering the game often heard from the guest side, while pounding on his clattering Smith-Corona, "Please hold it down, will you?"

After Victor died, the Morabito heirs inherited the franchise. Eventually, after the 49ers failed to win a championship over the next 12 seasons, the two heirs sold their interests to a wealthy construction builder from Youngstown, Ohio, named Edward DeBartolo Sr. for $17 million.

"They were right in that decision," said club president Lou Spadia. "That was their only source of income."

There were several other prospective buyers, including Wayne Valley who once owned a share of the Oakland Raiders, and Franklin Mieuli, who owned the Golden State Warriors basketball team. Then Raiders owner Al Davis, who had feuded with Mieuli over the years, got involved, leading the Morabito heirs to an unexpected buyer from across the country, one who had enough money to buy the entire league.

CHAPTER 1
DIFFERENT ROADS

"**O**PPOSITES ATTRACT." IT'S an old saying that usually applies to social circles. But Bill Walsh, a gifted football coach, and Edward DeBartolo Jr., the new owner of the San Francisco 49ers, took the meaning to a new level when they first met. Walsh stood 6-foot-5. He'd played tight end at San Jose State and was a lifetime football man. DeBartolo was probably a foot shorter and never played the game after a brief fling as a quarterback in grammar school.

Walsh's father grew up in the Great Depression and completed only the eighth grade. His mother dropped out of school after her junior year. The family sometimes lived in trailer parks in Southern California. DeBartolo's father, a Notre Dame graduate, was a billionaire contractor who purchased the 49ers for $17 million and gave the team to his son. And their hair: Walsh's was snow white, while DeBartolo's was as dark as midnight. Opposite as they were, they both shared a burning desire to turn the 49ers, a struggling, disorganized team playing in a city that had tragically lost its mayor and its pride, into a winner.

"He was a real blue-collar kid," said Craig Walsh of his father. "My grandfather painted cars in his spare time. My dad would help him with the projects. He wanted my dad to get into the custom-car painting business, because it was just taking off."

Coach Bill Walsh, quarterback Joe Montana, and owner Eddie DeBartolo celebrate the 49ers' first Super Bowl win.

It was a time when teenagers cruised the downtown streets of Los Angeles, looking for adventure in their flashy cars known as "hot rods." Walsh got caught up in the trend and the jazzy colors of the cars that thundered along the streets of Los Angeles, his birthplace. "He loved sanding cars and painting them," said Craig Walsh. "It was kind of a hobby back then."

It was also tedious work. Yet, Walsh never complained about rubbing cars down. "You learned a few details, because that was the kind of business it was. That was what was expected of me. So my dad gave me a work ethic, whether he meant to or not."

Accordingly, Walsh was always a man of detail. As a teenager, he worked on weekends for his father, who owned a small body-and-fender business outside of LA. "I would sand the cars and prepare them for painting," recalled Walsh. "I would assist him all day, and when the day was over, he'd give me a dollar."

Mike White, who coached briefly for the 49ers in 1979, recalled Walsh's challenging youth.

"I had met his mom and dad, and I knew his sister Maureen really well," he said. "When I met his parents, they were living in a trailer park down in Southern California. They were just good, solid, strong people. When his dad passed away, his mom moved to another trailer area. I don't mean that as a put-down. His parents weren't living in some 50-story mansion, smoking cigars. They were just hard-working, diligent people."

Despite his parents' struggle with money and education, Walsh took from them a sense of pride and self-motivation. They taught him the simplest of equations: hard, productive work equals success. Later, in the sport that defined his life, Walsh and the 240 players he coached during his 49er years lived by the Walsh family doctrine.

"I grew up in an ethnic neighborhood, just a cross-section of people, working people," said Walsh. "There was a movie house that some years later was the center of a big riot in Los Angeles. You walked to the movie because you were young and healthy. Later on I got my first car when I was 16, just after the war ended. It was a '34 Plymouth. We were just kids, and life was so much fun."

Walsh said he became fascinated by the game of football at a very early age. He always read the sports section of the *Los Angeles Times* and followed Southern California's team, "The school of my choice." He remembers watching the Trojans play their key games. "I became a big fan of USC," he said. "I saw the USC-Notre Dame game when Angelo Bertelli threw a touchdown pass for Notre Dame in a 13–0 win. So I was always interested in football. They had a kids' gate at the Coliseum where it cost 25 cents to get in. The seats were in a corner section. It was quite an afternoon."

In those younger years, Walsh played football in the street.

"We didn't have Pop Warner back then," he said. "If you wanted to play, you could get into a game of tackle with no pads whatsoever. I remember the first time I tackled a guy. I didn't have a helmet, or shoulder pads, or anything on. Both of us laid there thinking, *What the hell kind of game is this?*" Later, Walsh made his high school team as a freshman quarterback and threw three touchdown passes in one game. "Then I was a hot item," he recalled.

Because his father kept changing jobs, Walsh attended three high schools, one of them in Oregon.

"I played halfback on offense, and some defense," he said. "I had some interesting games at times, but never played great."

According to Walsh, he never intended to consider coaching as a profession.

"I was so bashful and self-conscious, I couldn't ever picture myself speaking in front of a group," he said. "I was scared to death." He never considered a tryout for any NFL team "because they had only 33 players per team and there wasn't any future in it. But the only adjunct to it was coaching.

"I got serious about being a coach when I was in the Army. I had time to reflect on it and mature. I had to mature because I got married to Geri, just before I went in the service."

Walsh enrolled at San Jose State, where he was a two-way end and came in contact with a coach named Bob Bronzan.

"His style of coaching, his technical knowledge," said Walsh. "He was ahead of everybody. He inspired me, all of his players . . . We won our share of games. We beat Arizona State and Brigham Young. We beat schools like that. I had a shoulder injury my senior year and missed four games, but still won two varsity letters. I really went to San Jose State because I was in love with a girl [Geri]. The coach didn't want to be bothered with a left-handed quarterback, so I was moved to end."

His first coaching job was at Fremont High School, where the starting salary was $4,650. His three assistants were all full-time teachers. Fremont had lost 27 straight games. The school had 750 kids who were mostly Hispanic, Portuguese, Spanish, and Asian. The school was located in a farming area.

"All of them were small, you know, 5-foot-9, 160 pounds," said Walsh, "and we played the best schools in that area."

Then Walsh got lucky. A freeway connecting Oakland with San Jose was finished. Another 750 students from new housing developments enrolled at his high school, and suddenly Walsh was coaching 6-foot, 200-pounders. Fremont started to win games with its bigger, stronger teams.

"We were winning, and I thought it was me," said Walsh. "But it was the freeway. We beat the conference champs in our first game 11–0, and we went on to have good years. Then one year we won all of our games to finish 9–0."

* * *

Eddie DeBartolo, grew up in Youngstown, Ohio, a largely ethnic town located 65 miles southeast of Cleveland and 61 miles northwest of Pittsburgh.

"Youngstown is a very unusual town," said DeBartolo, who still visits his birthplace. "It is a strong ethnic town. It was the type of town that made you a better person. It was a very, very tough town. There was a lot of criminal activity, there were a lot of people in town who were unsavory. If you were able to survive and be successful, that was really saying something."

Although he lives in Tampa, Florida, DeBartolo still regards Youngstown as his true home.

"It's home, and nothing's changed, yet everything's changed," he said. "I come home and I look where I used to live, the two or three houses where I was brought up. There's no place like home. It's a saying that's used very often, but it's true."

DeBartolo's father, who would become a billionaire in the construction business after World War II, was born in Youngstown. His parents, Anthony Paonessa and Rose Villari, immigrated from Italy. After

Anthony's death, Rose remarried and Edward the junior took his step-father's family name.

"After the war, my dad started working with my grandfather building roads," said Eddie. "Then he started building strip centers in Cleveland and Pittsburgh. I vividly remember driving with him to various projects and construction sites when I was six or seven years old. My father got into the mall business at just the right time, just when America was ready for something new, an *evolutionary* development."

In his preteen years, Eddie played football with a grammar school, leading his team to a championship in 1958.

"Then I tried out for the team at Cardinal Mooney High School, and I wasn't very good," he said. "I couldn't make the team. I played for about three weeks on the taxi squad. Then I quit because I realized I would rather spend my time with girls, because I was never going to be any good at football."

In the summers, he worked in the construction and maintenance departments of his father's company.

"I began at the bottom, shoveling snow and mowing lawns at the Youngstown Mall," said Eddie. "When I got older, I went into the office. We had different departments, and each summer I would work in a different department. One summer in the legal department, another summer in real estate. I was bouncing around the office, trying to learn as much as I could. I made a lot of trips with [my dad]. I just grew with the company and ended up becoming the president and CEO."

Eddie described his father's work ethic as "unbelievable." Edward Sr. kept a plaque on his desk that he referred to for inspiration. It contained a famous verse written by Amanda Bradley.

The DeBartolo Company began building fashionable malls directly after the end of World War II. Eddie would accompany his father on his private plane to search for potential mall locations.

"He had this uncanny ability to pick locations, to know where the growth was going to come," said Eddie. "Then we'd go down and negotiate for a certain amount of acreage for a shopping mall. That's how it all started. At one time we had 110 shopping malls. We had about 800 people working in Youngstown."

Eddie says he learned to work long days from his father, for whom a 17-hour day was normal.

"His work ethic was unparalleled," said Eddie. "I hope some of it has passed on and passed in through me. I get up at 4:30 or 5:00 a.m. every morning. And I try to work out, but I've got this bad hip, fluid on it. I don't need a replacement. It just kind of curtails me from working out." DeBartolo underwent back surgery in 2018 to alleviate his pain, a 45-minute procedure that left him sore but rejuvenated.

When Eddie feels like drifting away from some project, he recalls one of his father's favorite lines and plunges back into the job.

"My wife has never seen me lie down when the sun was up," he once told his senior executives. Eddie also learned the value of a family dinner.

"He was a five o'clock man," said Eddie of his father. "He'd be at the office at 5:00 or 5:30 and he'd work until the dinner hour. We would always be home by six o'clock or 6:15. He made sure no matter where we traveled that we'd always be home for dinner."

CHAPTER 2

THE MEETING THAT
CHANGED HISTORY

THE FIRST LINE of Amanda Bradley's verse that Eddie DeBartolo's father used for inspiration focused on the desire to be a dreamer. Early in 1979, after his father had purchased the San Francisco 49ers franchise for $17 million and turned the team over to his 30-year-old son, Eddie was also inspired to dream. He began thinking of hiring Don Shula as his first head coach.

"I really tried to convince Don Shula," Eddie said, "but he was entrenched in Miami with his family, and obviously the Dolphins, so that didn't happen."

Shula had coached the Dolphins for nine seasons, winning two Super Bowls, one of which produced the league's only perfect season (17–0). So Eddie's dream ended before it really started.

Shula doesn't recall any conversation with DeBartolo.

"I don't remember doing it," he said. "I just remember what a fine coach Bill Walsh was."

There were a number of experienced coaches available for DeBartolo: Ron Erhardt, Tom Flores, and Ray Perkins, all of whom became head coaches that year, and a couple of New York Giants assistants, Bill

Belichick and Bill Parcells. Only DeBartolo had no list. He watched the Bluebonnet Bowl on New Year's Eve in which Bill Walsh's Stanford team rallied from a 22–0 deficit to defeat Georgia.

"That's what sold me," DeBartolo said. "I told my dad, 'I really have to try and interview this man.' I said, 'I've heard a lot about him. In the Bay Area, I've heard about what a good person he was and a great coach and how innovative he was. Also the problems, the trouble he had in Cincinnati, where he obviously wanted that head coaching job that was given to Tiger Johnson.'"

In the Bluebonnet Bowl, Walsh gave a stirring halftime speech, only to have Georgia score on their first second-half possession to open a 22-point lead.

"It was a credit to the players and coaches that we were able to keep our composure," Walsh later said. "Not panicking, we were finally able to adjust to their eight-man fronts and pressure package with our quick passes and 'hot' adjustments. It was an excellent springboard to the challenge of taking on the San Francisco 49ers."

Carmen Policy, the attorney for the DeBartolo company in Youngstown who joined the 49ers as an executive, remembers the Shula story like some old legal case.

"You know things went very badly the first two years," he said. "Eddie was literally torn to pieces by the media and by the fans. Things were getting personal. They were ridiculing him and Joe Thomas, the general manager. Keep in mind, Eddie was only 30 years old when his father bought the team. Think of that. Thirty years old."

DeBartolo then decided to take charge. "He decided he was going to get rid of Joe Thomas and the coach [Pete McCulley]," said Policy. "He was going to clean up the front office and really try to remake the entire franchise."

Policy said that DeBartolo "kind of liked" Bill Walsh. "But Edward Sr. had checked with several people in the league. And he was getting feedback from Paul Brown [Cincinnati's owner], Joe Robbie [Miami's owner], and others, including the Nordstroms [Seattle Seahawks owners], and the word was that Bill Walsh was not emotionally tough enough to handle it and that he had some other demons. Everybody came to Senior [DeBartolo] and said, 'If you really want to change what's happening out there, you ought to hire Don Shula.' But Shula had already won two Super Bowls and had a perfect season, so why would he want to leave Miami?"

Eddie decided to ignore all the critics and doomsday cynics and invited Walsh to a meeting at his condo atop fashionable Nob Hill, not far from San Francisco's luxurious Fairmont Hotel.

"I thought it was important to have a new coach in place and a new organization in place prior to the draft," said DeBartolo.

Eddie asked Policy to join him and handle any contract discussion. Learning of his son's plan, the senior DeBartolo called Policy into his office in Youngstown.

"This was done without Eddie's knowledge," said Policy, "He tried to sabotage the deal. He said, 'My son is making a big mistake. I'm hearing from people who know the game, and they're saying this guy is not the right guy to be a head coach.'

"One of the most influential people who had DeBartolo Sr.'s ear was Oakland Raiders owner Al Davis. He told Senior, 'You need a football guy there to guide Eddie, and there's no better football guy than Joe Thomas."

DeBartolo said that Walsh wanted "not only talented players, but players who could think on their feet. He wanted players who were smart, not only football smart, but also book smart. That's the way he operated."

According to DeBartolo, the meeting with Walsh lasted only 40 to 45 minutes. It started with what DeBartolo called "a little chit-chat, a little bit of this and that, and then about the bowl game. Then, believe it or not, we talked about 'family.' I told him about how we ran our business in Youngstown. How everyone was considered part of the family. He told me about his family. Then we talked about philosophy. He talked about his innovations and his very bad experience with the Bengals. He was not happy. There was just something that I saw in this man."

DeBartolo switched back to the broad topic of family values.

"I want the franchise built and run with the same approach we take with the company," he said. "Can we do it in football? Can we do it the same way we've done it with our development and construction company in Youngstown?"

"Definitely," said Walsh. "And I can see how it could be very beneficial to the team."

Policy remembers the very first time he saw Walsh. "When he walked into Eddie's condo, his presence filled the room. You know, I had never met Bill before that meeting. He was just so impressive. The way he handled himself, the things he said. You know, when we had that meeting in Eddie's condo, Bill came in through the delivery entrance. Eddie talked about all the stuff that Eddie wanted to hear. He hired him that night."

Policy thought the meeting lasted longer than Eddie recalled.

"I think the meeting went on for about an hour and a half, and then we spent another 45 minutes drinking champagne," he said. "I know because I knew what time it was back in Youngstown. It was almost midnight in San Francisco.

"DeBartolo talked about the organization and what kind of people he was going to bring in to run the 49ers. It was really uplifting," Policy continued. "Now, keep in mind, Eddie had met Bill before. So this was going to be the final interview to determine if Bill was going to be the guy he was going to hire."

Walsh received a four-year contract that started at $220,000, with escalators of $50,000 each year.

Eddie DeBartolo proved to be much more than just an owner with the deepest pockets in the league. Policy often described him as "fiery," recalling a game in which the 49ers blew a lead and lost to the New Orleans Saints. DeBartolo entered the Superdome dressing room, picked up a wooden stool, and hurled it at a nearby soda machine, shattering its glass front.

Defensive back Ronnie Lott shook his head at the damage.

Owner Eddie DeBartolo and Coach Bill Walsh had their differences but shared a burning desire to win.

"What happened?" he asked Policy, who pointed to Eddie.

"What's the matter, Mr. D, didn't you have a quarter?"

There would be times when the owner and his head coach would clash. Family values would temporarily be forgotten and the air would be filled with anger and disbelief.

"At times he felt Bill was slacking off and not doing the job he should be doing as a coach, and he was right," said Policy. "Bill went through periods when he almost became depressed, you know. He didn't have that toughness, that personality that Parcells or Lombardi or Shula had and Belichick has. And that's exactly what the critics were thinking about. They weren't thinking that he wasn't intelligent enough. They just didn't see any of that toughness in Bill. They thought he wouldn't last very many seasons with the ups and downs a coach has to deal with."

Bill Walsh not only survived, he proved to be the perfect coach for the struggling 49ers and their city of dreamers. Who would have thought that three years after the meeting with Walsh, 2,082 miles and two time zones away the 49ers would win their first Super Bowl? The critics would vanish like those flutes of champagne that DeBartolo, Walsh, and Policy consumed on that historic night on Nob Hill—and a city torn by murders and anger would rejoice as the confetti floated through the bright lights on that winter evening in a domed stadium in suburban Detroit known as the Silverdome.

Over the years, watching the skilled players and playing referee whenever DeBartolo and Walsh had their "family arguments," Policy said the experience was almost overwhelming.

"It was beyond a helluva experience," he said. "It was a blessing to be part of it. Just to be part of an organization and a lifestyle that included those men with those talents and those personalities and the competition that existed at that level. Waking up every morning, you realize that you're part of it. It was electric and you lived with it, every single day of the week. It was unbelievably exciting."

CHAPTER 3

THE DREAMER WHO MADE IT ALL POSSIBLE

HE WAS THE rock of the family. A huge rock. He was also a dreamer, a visionary and a workaholic whose long days inspired the line, "My wife has never seen me lying down when the sun was up."

Edward DeBartolo Sr. graduated from Notre Dame with a degree in civil engineering, so he knew all about sports. At Notre Dame, you automatically fall in love with the sporting life. So he took that affection to an extreme. In 1977, he purchased the San Francisco 49ers, a National Football League team, for his son Eddie Jr. That same year he bought the Pittsburgh Penguins of the National Hockey League and placed his daughter, Denise, in charge of operations.

DeBartolo made his fortune after World War II. His parents had immigrated from Italy and settled in Youngstown, Ohio. He established the Edward J. DeBartolo Corporation and began building roads and strip malls. Working 15-hour days, DeBartolo enlarged his company until it was the unchallenged leader in building shopping malls from Tampa to Tacoma; at one count, the DeBartolo Company had constructed 110 malls. DeBartolo operated his business by stressing family values, the joy or illness of one member to be embraced by management and the other workers. It was this love for one another that his son transferred to the 49ers.

DeBartolo's tight relationship with his company became a topic during his son's hiring interview with Bill Walsh. Eddie felt that this bonding as a group could create a very special team if the affection was real and not left on the practice field.

"It can work," Walsh told the young owner, "and it can help us with the players as we start rebuilding the team. It might even spread around the league."

Walsh's idea of creating a family atmosphere among the youthful 49ers extended to every department and every job, from players and coaches to scouting departments and the financial office, ticket sellers and ball boys. Soon, even Eddie's father, who had been opposed to hiring Walsh, caught the family spirit and work ethic of the 49ers and embraced what his son had accomplished.

"I think he grew to like me," said Walsh. "I looked like a coach. And I think he was weary at that point that he had a hard time trusting all those other sources because he had been led down the wrong path. So I was a welcome relief, a sense of humor, and not affected by all that criticism."

"When Eddie and I first became friends, we were in our twenties," said Carmen Policy, DeBartolo's attorney who joined the 49ers as an executive. "He had just graduated from Notre Dame, and I was a young prosecutor. I started doing some work for Mr. DeBartolo and the family, and then the corporation. Mr. DeBartolo was an amazing, amazing man. He grew up the old-fashioned way. His mother put him on a bus to Notre Dame and told him, 'Don't come back until you have an engineering degree.'"

Because of his engineering skills, DeBartolo served in the Army Corps of Engineers in Okinawa during World War II. He married Marie Montani in 1944 and founded the Edward J. DeBartolo Corporation soon after his discharge. With a gifted sense that foresaw young postwar families moving to the suburbs, DeBartolo began his incredible rise as a construction tycoon by paving roads and building houses, shopping centers, and strip malls.

"He came up with this idea of people are starting to want to live in the suburbs, so let's put a group of stores together and create a little strip center," said Policy. "He did that in an outskirt of Youngstown called Boardman, and that catapulted into the shopping center industry."

Policy remembers DeBartolo as a driven man.

"Oh, he was up early, early in the morning," said Policy. "He worked all day long, always in a three-piece suit with a tie."

"He was very classy, very sophisticated," said Walsh. "He was quiet, but he had a lot of command to his presence. He dressed impeccably. He was just a very unique man."

As a young man, DeBartolo owned several small planes.

"He didn't fly them, but he loved aircraft," said Policy. "Then he got a Lear." DeBartolo flew those planes to locate potential areas for his shopping malls.

"He was all about discipline and work," said Policy. "And I'll never, ever forget what he taught me when Eddie and I were running around together. He said, 'I'm never going to tell you not to play. But I'm going to tell you this. Make sure you're working harder than you play. Okay, you want to come home at two or three o'clock in the morning? Make sure you're up at five and ready to go to work.'"

All through those formative years, Eddie began to understand some of his family's Italian-American culture.

"He was the first-born and he was the son," said Policy. "And to Senior, Eddie was beyond special. Now, he recognized that his son could be problematic in terms of controlling. But he adored Eddie. You know, I don't know if Senior's life would have been nearly as special if he hadn't had Eddie in it. And Eddie had an amazing, amazing respect and admiration for his father."

As a Notre Damer, DeBartolo Sr. grew to love the competitive aspect of major sports, notably football. "He was a sportsman, just as his son was," remembered Policy.

Bill Walsh remembered DeBartolo as a smart, shrewd businessman.

DeBartolo founded the Pittsburgh Maulers of the young United States Football League in 1983, six years after buying the 49ers. But when the USFL announced it planned to move to a fall schedule, meaning it would challenge the established NFL, DeBartolo disbanded the team. In 1977, he purchased the Pittsburgh Penguins, an established National Hockey League team, for his daughter, Denise. DeBartolo also entered the sport of soccer, buying the Pittsburgh Spirit indoor team. His interest in horse racing led to the ownership of three race tracks: Louisiana Downs, Thistledown, and Remington Park. (When horse racing began to struggle in the 1990s, son-in-law John York sold all three struggling tracks.)

Before Denise and her husband took control of the team in 2000, the 49ers were an extension of the DeBartolo organization just as Eddie and Bill Walsh had discussed in their first meeting.

Groundbreaking for the 49ers' new stadium in Santa Clara.

"I think we were the best organization in football," said Walsh. "We paid a lot of attention to detail. We took a more comprehensive look at everything and plotted where we were going. We had some marvelous people working with us, right down the line. Our coaching staff. The management people. And there was central leadership. That's what made us so effective."

CHAPTER 4

A QUARTERBACK NAMED JOE COOL

ALMOST FROM THE time that he could pick up a football, Joe Montana was blessed with teachers who knew about the basics of playing quarterback. The quick drop back. The snappy delivery of the football, nose up, then down into the receiver's hands. And always a soft, catchable ball.

Montana's teachers included his father, Joe Sr.; Carl Crawley, his Pop Warner coach; and Paul Zolak, his coach at Ringgold High School in Monongahela, Pennsylvania.

"Joe's father was a big influence," Zolak told sportswriter Ray Didinger. "He worked with Joe after school, practicing techniques. I remember one summer day when he pitched in an American Legion baseball game. After the game was over, everyone headed for the Dairy Queen except for Joe and his father. They stayed in the outfield where his father had Joe working on his quarterback steps—three-step [drop], five-step, seven-step, so he'd be ready for football."

"I wish I could take credit for Joe's success, but I can't," said Crawley. "You can't take a junker and turn it into a luxury car. Joe had so much ability it was easy to coach him. He was a quick learner, and he just loved to play. Joe had a feel for competitive things that was very unusual. I told him, 'If you're the quarterback, you'll have to call the play. And you have to know why you're calling it.' I remember talking over down-and-distance situations with him, and here's Joe, nine years old, absorbing it all."

Years later, when Montana was auditioning for the San Francisco 49ers a week before the 1979 NFL Draft, offensive coordinator Sam Wyche would be impressed by the same basics.

"Joe threw the ball beautifully," said Wyche. "When you throw, you want the front of the ball nose up. And when it comes down, you want the nose down. I just made a mental note that Joe wasn't going to have a lot of dropped passes. He put the ball right where the receiver could catch it. Nice and soft. And the way he released the ball. He threw a real tight spiral."

Bill Walsh was also impressed. Steve Dils, the quarterback Walsh had coached at Stanford, was among a thin crop of quarterbacks in that year's draft.

"The first time I saw Joe drop from center," Walsh said, "I said to myself, *This is Namath*. Those quick, nimble feet. Almost like a ballet dancer's feet. So fluid. He was ideally suited to the offense I wanted to run."

According to Tony Razzano (as told in his book *Secrets of an NFL Scout*), who had just joined the 49ers as a director of scouting, "Bill was eager to take Dils, even after Montana's impressive hour-long workout a week before the NFL draft." Razzano insisted that Walsh and Wyche held the pre-draft workout for James Owens, a UCLA back with brilliant speed. The plan was to draft Owens in the second round and convert him into a wide receiver. The 49ers had given away their first-round pick to Buffalo for an aging running back named O. J. Simpson.

"Walsh went to see James Owens, and Montana just happened to be there," said Razzano in his book. "Bill was not sold that Montana was his man. Sam Wyche felt the same way."

Razzano revealed that early in the draft, Walsh asked the player personnel director John Ralston to call Notre Dame coach Dan Devine to get his opinion on Montana. Devine couldn't think of any negatives. "So Walsh agreed to take Montana," said Razzano. "But in the back of his mind you could that Bill was not happy, almost as if he were sure he could get Dils, too."

When the fourth round came, the Vikings took Dils. Razzano, assuming the 49ers had a fourth-round pick, claimed that Walsh slammed his fist on his desk and cursed, "Dammit, I knew we should have taken Steve Dils in the third round." (In actuality, the 49ers didn't have a fourth-round choice, having traded it to the Bills in the Simpson deal.)

Wyche, Walsh's offensive coordinator, also disputes Razzano's version of how the 49ers' draft strategy played out. According to him, Walsh asked him to find a quarterback to throw to Owens in his pre-draft workout at UCLA.

"I knew Joe was staying in Manhattan Beach, so I called and got him to come," said Wyche. "We thought Owens could be another Charlie Joiner type of receiver. Joiner caught 750 passes in his Hall of Fame career with Houston, Cincinnati, and San Diego.

"Joe threw the ball beautifully," recalled Wyche. "The way he released the ball. The wrist action. The nose of the ball was up. I knew Bill had Dils at Stanford and he knew him as a quarterback who would fit into his system. But Joe came along and we got a good read on him. Bill changed his mind right away. Owens had a mediocre workout. He dropped some balls. On draft day, there wasn't a person in that room who didn't want Joe. Bill and I got on the plane the night after the workout and we both agreed: We would take Owens on the second round and Montana on the third. Nobody knew at the time how good he was going to be."

In checking around the league, Walsh found that no other team had rated Montana higher than the fourth round.

"We took him in the third and were criticized for taking him that high," said Walsh. The concerns for most teams was Montana's size as a pro quarterback and how he would survive the pounding from those huge, quick pass rushers. Some scouts also questioned his modest arm strength. Montana is listed at 6-feet-2 on most rosters. Actually, he's closer to 6 feet and a half- inch.

"But Joe has an instinct for the game," noted Walsh. "He has an ability to make spontaneous plays that can't be measured and can't be coached. The great quarterbacks have it, and Joe had it to a degree that I feel is unmatched in the history of the game."

The saddest scout on the day of the 1979 draft had to be Red Cochran, who evaluated college talent for the Green Bay Packers. Cochran all but begged Packers coach Bart Starr, a Hall of Fame quarterback, to draft Montana.

"They asked me what would happen if we didn't take him," said Cochran, as conveyed in the *NFL Draft Encyclopedia*. "I said, 'I'm going to throw up and walk out of the room.'" When the Packers took two running backs, Eddie Lee Ivery and Steve Atkins, in the first two rounds, then bypassed Montana eleven spots above the 49ers, Cochran bolted from the draft room. "I didn't throw up, but I walked out of the room," he fumed.

The Packers' choice was Charles Johnson, a defensive tackle from Maryland who lasted only three seasons.

"We had started counting down," said Cochran. "I knew only a couple of teams that needed quarterbacks. When I got within three teams, I knew none of them wanted a quarterback. I said, 'We're going to get this, he's ours.' But Bart Starr had other ideas and took Johnson.

"We called up the Maryland coach and asked him about this Johnson kid," said Cochran. "I had rejected both of these guys [Johnson and Atkins], but what's a coach going to say. He had to say 'Yes,' so we drafted Johnson."

***

The area outside of Pittsburgh has produced a succession of outstanding quarterbacks: Joe Namath, George Blanda, Jim Kelly, Dan Marino, Jim Kelly, John Unitas, and Montana.

"Kids who grew up here are aware of the legacy," said Paul Zolak, Montana's former high school coach. "There is a love of sport that's handed down, generation to generation, especially football. It's nothing for a high school game to draw 10,000 people on a Friday night, I've talked to [NFL] players who played in other parts of the country where they had 200 or 300 people at their high school games. But here the kids thrive on it. All the best athletes want to play football, and the very best want to play quarterback."

Steve DeBerg, who would play 17 seasons and throw 5,024 passes for six different teams, was Bill Walsh's first starting quarterback. It was DeBerg's fate to play with an assortment of 49ers castoffs and youngsters through back-to-back 2–14 seasons in 1978 and '79. Early in the 1980 season, the 49ers were playing the New York Jets. DeBerg had developed laryngitis, so he was wearing a voice amplifier. But early in the game, DeBerg indicated he was having trouble communicating with his offense. Walsh sent in Montana, who ran a bootleg for a 5-yard touchdown.

As it turned out, there was nothing wrong with DeBerg's voice box. The whole procedure had been planned by Walsh, who wanted to give Montana some game experience.

"It shouldn't have taken a rocket scientist to realize Joe was going to run a bootleg," said veteran guard Randy Cross. "But the Jets couldn't figure it out."

Later that same season, the 49ers were taking a pounding in the trenches, as well as on the scoreboard, in a rain-drenched home game against the New Orleans Saints, the score reached 35–7 at halftime, yet Montana kept his cool, throwing to Dwight Clark and Freddie Solomon. He threw for two touchdowns and ran for another during a 28-point second-half outburst that pulled out a 38–35 overtime win.

Hall of Fame quarterback Joe Montana, who won four Super Bowls for the 49ers without throwing a single interception.

"This was the beginning of things for us," said Montana. "It really built our confidence."

Walsh already had planned on easing Montana into the lineup in his second season. That meant the end of DeBerg's rocky career with the 49ers—but he didn't leave easily.

"Steve DeBerg might have been the most competitive person I've ever known," said Cross, "and he brought that out in Joe. Putting these two together was like mixing napalm with nitroglycerine." Walsh eventually made two trades, sending DeBerg to Denver and obtaining Guy Benjamin, his quarterback at Stanford, to be Montana's backup.

"I can't put my finger on it," said Sam Wyche, "but there's something about Joe that draws you to him. He makes such a great leader.

I didn't say he's got the strongest arm around. But it's good enough. He's got the timing down. He has terrific anticipation. The thing about Joe is that he throws a very accurate ball that arrives very softly. You've got to be smart. You've got to be accurate. If you're not, there's no question: You're no NFL quarterback."

***

Some of the greatest quarterbacks finish their careers in strange places. Johnny Unitas played his last season in San Diego after a Hall of Fame career in Baltimore. Joe Namath threw his final pass for the Los Angeles Rams. And leave it to Jim McMahon to set the unofficial record for transfers: five different teams following a Super Bowl championship with the Chicago Bears.

Montana would be on the move, too, when he began suffering back and elbow injuries and Steve Young, the quarterback that Walsh had stolen from Tampa Bay with the help of Eddie DeBartolo's bank account and some smooth talking, began to replace him, initially during the 1987–'90 seasons, but especially in 1991 and '92. (Montana had suffered a significant injury to his elbow during the 1990 NFC Championship Game against the New York Giants, one severe enough to take him out of the 1991 season.)

In April 1993, the 49ers traded Montana to the Kansas City Chiefs. Montana's No. 16 had been worn with such distinction by the Chiefs' Len Dawson that it had been retired, so Montana settled for No. 19, worn by Cotton Davidson, a punter and the first starting quarterback for the American Football League's Dallas Texans. (The AFL Dallas Texans moved to Kansas City in 1963, where it became the Chiefs, eventually merging with the NFL.)

There were tears in San Francisco when the Montana trade was announced, some of them shed in the owner's office. But Steve Young gave the city some great years, too. He was younger than Montana, possessed the same snappy delivery and tough demeanor, and he added another dimension: he was a strong, natural runner.

Parting with Montana was especially tough on DeBartolo, with whom the quarterback had maintained a close relationship.

"Every player starts his career believing you'll never leave the team you're on," said Montana. "But eventually it happens to everyone. I never thought you'd see Jerry Rice play somewhere else. I would rather have stayed in San Francisco. I made the best of it."

Montana said DeBartolo allowed him to make the final decision. Always the ultimate competitor, Montana elected to continue his career with the Chiefs. And on a Sunday of twisted emotions in 1994, he led the Chiefs to a 24–17 win over Steve Young and the 49ers.

"Eddie probably was torn," said Montana. "I wasn't. I wanted to win. I'm sure Eddie did, too, but I'm sure a little piece of him was torn. It was hard. If he had to lose one, he was probably all right with that one."

One of the dissenters regarding the trade was Dwight Clark, Montana's clutch receiver.

"I couldn't believe they wanted to trade Joe Montana," said Clark. "I understood the money, but how could you do that to a four-time Super Bowl champion? I wasn't in favor of it. For five or six years, he [Montana] and I didn't talk very much, and he was my best friend. I had to make sure he knew I wasn't any part of that."

CHAPTER 5
THE WEST COAST OFFENSE

THERE IS STILL speculation about how the short, rhythmic passing scheme, with its three- and five-step quarterback drops, came to be known as the "West Coast offense." Sure, most of the pass-minded teachers that Walsh knew early in his career were associated with West Coast teams, notably Sid Gillman, Don Coryell, and Al Davis. Yet Walsh's early coaching years were in Cincinnati as the offensive coordinator for the legendary Paul Brown. It was Walsh who turned the Bengals into an offensive threat at a time when most teams were using the standard formula to get to the Super Bowl: a smart quarterback who threw high-percentage passes; a 1,000-yard back; and an aggressive, big-play defense that flew to the ball and knocked down quarterbacks. The 1972 Super Bowl champion Miami Dolphins were the model.

Yet, Walsh persisted in using the short, quick pass on any down as the key to his offense. He also almost never deviated from the West Coast makeup: two backs and three receivers, with the quarterback always under center, rather than in a shotgun set with the quarterback five yards deep.

According to Walsh, "The most important principle is a willingness to pass on first down. You have to complete a bigger percentage of your passes in this offense than most teams can. You're trying to keep possession throwing the ball. You're trying to move down the field—and the best way to do that is with closely-timed, short- to medium-range passes."

Walsh also felt that the West Coast offense forced other teams to keep their base defense on the field, with three linebackers and four defensive backs, instead of situation specialists.

"So you attack them with a base set that threatens everything, everywhere, on every down," he said. "That means a possession receiver, a speed receiver, a good receiving tight end who is also a very good blocker, and two running backs who are also good receivers. In the pure West Coast offense, there are very few plays with four wide receivers, or even three."

While the West Coast system seems to focus on the early pass, Walsh insists that this isn't true. "No, our objective is to establish the offense," he said. "On first down, we want to establish that we can move the ball either passing or running. That means being ready, willing, and able to do either. The big thing on first down isn't throwing, it's a *willingness* to throw. What it takes is a sound way to throw the ball that will make the assistant coaches, as well as the players, feel confident that they can do it."

Some pro teams appear reluctant to open up with the pass, preferring to play it cozy and play down-and-distance offense, but, said Walsh, "[F]irst down is the one time when the defense can't gear up against passes. On first down, they always have to be ready for the run, too."

A common criticism about Walsh's offense was that it was a dink-and-dunk scheme that rarely uses the deep pass. Walsh disagreed. "We call as many long passes as any other team," he said. "We might call a particular deep pass and throw it once or five times and not throw it at all. What we do in every game is go to the outlet receiver quicker than other teams. If the deep pass isn't open right now, we go immediately to the tight end or a back."

Walsh said that one factor in using the West Coast scheme is the size and quickness of the defensive linemen and linebackers on running plays that they anticipate. "They're too quick and mobile," he said. "When was the last time you saw an offensive line block seven guys to the ground? A well-designed pass offense is more reliable for ball control.

"Look, if a team is trying to establish the run, charged-up defensive players will climb through good blockers to get your ballcarrier. And there goes your running game. But pass offense is skill, not muscle. An effective pass offense neutralizes muscle. That's one of the great things about it. When you leave your base defense on the field, with the quarterback under center, the defense has to account for every run and pass you have on every down."

The West Coast scheme, now a part of every NFL playbook, includes power plays, traps, sweeps, draws, quick passes, and deep passes.

"We're not against formations with four or five wide receivers," said Walsh, "provided you're using them for either of two reasons: to see if the defense makes a poor adjustment or gives you a major mismatch. But we think it's counterproductive to bring in three or four wide receivers just to confuse the defense by giving them a different look. That's because timing is so critical to pass offense. And the more people milling about, the harder it is to get your timing down."

Bill McPherson, the defensive coordinator under Walsh, sometimes would get frustrated during practice sessions.

"It was a masterful system," said McPherson. "Bill had it down to a science."

Indeed, the system was so quick and rhythmic that McPherson's defense sometimes bristled in practice sessions when the ball hardly ever touched the ground.

Mike Holmgren, who coached Walsh's offense from 1986 to 1991, said, "There was an old adage that you must run the ball . . . you must run the ball to win. Run the ball, play defense, teach toughness. All those sorts of things. So throwing the ball in place of running it was different. Then there was the thought that if you threw the ball, you couldn't develop a toughness, that it was more of a finesse, trick-type thing. But with the 49ers, we had our share of tough, physical players."

In Walsh's scheme, the offensive linemen were the lightest in the league with one exception: 315-pound tackle Bubba Paris.

"Bill believed, as did his line coach Bob McKittrick, that he wanted smart, athletic linemen," said Holmgren. "Bubba Paris was by far our biggest lineman. But he [Walsh] wanted quick, athletic linemen to do what he wanted to get done."

"So many teams use variations of it," said former Dallas coach Jimmy Johnson. "A little bit of this, a little bit of that. All 32 teams use some parts of it."

Lynn Stiles, a 49ers assistant, said the offense always "practiced quick and fast. Sometimes the ball never touched the ground."

So, was it Walsh's "masterful system" that was the foundation for five Super Bowls? Or was it the superb quarterback play of Joe Montana and Steve Young, coupled with an underrated 49ers defense? Holmgren talked about the importance of having Montana and then Young at the position.

"Our offensive system is a great system, but to make that thing really work the best, you have to have a great quarterback. If he has a bad day, you team is not going to do really well. Now, we've had Joe and Steve and, for a stretch, Steve Bono came in and did a marvelous job. Offensively, what's helped, too, is that for years the nucleus of that team has been there. You had John Taylor, Jerry Rice, and Brent Jones. [In the backfield] it was Roger Craig and Tom Rathman, and up front, [Steve] Wallace, [Harris] Barton, [Jesse] Sapolu . . . seven or eight guys who played in that system for a long time and who are very talented guys." Even today, when 49ers fans remember those very special seasons at Candlestick, the debate continues.

So does the mystique of the term "West Coast offense." As Walsh pointed out, Cincinnati isn't a coastal city, and it is many miles from the Pacific Coast. Maybe the term came from an unlikely source. Former pro quarterback Bernie Kosar, ending his career with the Dallas Cowboys, once told a friend, "They're using some of that West Coast stuff here."

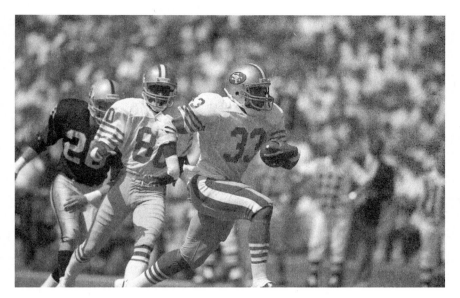

Running back Roger Craig gave the 49ers a solid running game.

The scheme began spreading to other NFL teams when they watched tapes of Walsh's offense after he became Paul Brown's coordinator with the Bengals. In 1970, the Bengals' quarterback was Virgil Carter, who was more dangerous with his legs than his passing arm. Yet Walsh developed the Bengals into the second-best offense in the AFC, scoring more points than Joe Namath's New York Jets.

Most fans figured the short, rhythmic passing game was another of Brown's innovations. After all, Brown had given pro football its open huddle, with his film study, classroom instruction, and messenger guards to carry plays to the quarterback. Although Walsh called the plays from the coach's box, many fans and television viewers felt Brown was responsible for play-calling after seeing him huddle with his messenger guard on the sideline. In reality, it was Walsh who would relay the play to an assistant, who would then send the call to Brown on the sideline.

"It was the most inefficient, cumbersome procedure imaginable," said Walsh. "But it preserved the fiction that Paul was pulling the strings. He wasn't even sure what the system was."

Brown, a football lifer, decided to resign after the 1975 season in which the Bengals finished 11–3 and sent quarterback Ken Anderson to the Pro Bowl. In the Walsh years, three receivers—tight end Bob Trumpy and wideouts Isaac Curtis and Chip Myers—became Pro Bowlers. At the end of their best season, it almost seemed logical that Brown would select Walsh as his successor. Brown, however, named offensive line coach Bill Johnson. (Three years later, after a 0–5 start—in a dreadful season for the Bengals that ended 4–12—in which the Bengals' offense scored 66 points, Johnson left the team.)

"When push came to shove, Paul just couldn't bring himself to turn it over to me," said Walsh. "There was something like jealousy involved, mixed with a kind of resentment. Sometimes I didn't think I could live through it. I was truly broken. It was crushing. I was very, very lost."

There were seven other head coaching jobs available after that 1976 season. Some of the teams called Brown to inquire about Walsh. Each of them got the same negative message: Brown felt Walsh was too emotional to handle the highs and lows of the game.

Years later, after Walsh's young, aggressive 49ers had beaten the Bengals in Super Bowl XVI, Brown stepped down from his pedestal and apologized to the winning coach. "I was wrong, Bill," he said. "I was wrong."

Records of Head Coaches Hired in 1976 When Bill Walsh Was Passed over after Retiring and Cincinnati Coach Paul Brown Failed to Give Him a Recommendation

- Buffalo—Jim Ringo, 3–20
- Cincinnati—Bill Johnson, 18–15
- New York Jets—Lou Holtz, 3–10
- New Orleans—Hank Stram 7–21
- New York Giants—John McVay, 14–23
- Philadelphia—Dick Vermeil, 57–51
- San Francisco—Monte Clark, 8–6
- Seattle—Jack Patera, 35–59
- Tampa Bay—John McKay, 45–91–1

CHAPTER 6
START OF A DYNASTY

WHEN YOU HIT rock bottom in the NFL, the only reward is a chance to select higher in the next NFL draft. The year before Bill Walsh arrived, the 49ers had played under two head coaches and won only two games, one of them a 6–3 squeaker over Tampa Bay, an expansion team, and earned that higher pick.

But the 49ers inadvertently fumbled away their top pick, James Owens, a very fast running back from UCLA, when they got the chance to improve the team in the draft going into the 1979 season. The idea was to convert Owens into a wide receiver and kickoff returner; Owens, however, never developed and was gone after two forgettable seasons. Indeed, it was a lean 49ers draft that year, except for third-rounder Joe Montana and tenth-rounder Dwight Clark. Montana was the fourth quarterback drafted, Clark the twenty-fourth wide receiver and the overall two hundred forty-ninth selection.

While Walsh had already projected Montana as his new quarterback, there was no assurance for Clark. Indeed, scouts refer to low-rounders as "camp receivers," pass catchers who assure that starters have fresh legs in the summer heat. Clark had been almost an afterthought, scouted while Walsh was evaluating Steve Fuller, Clark's quarterback at Clemson.

Two seasons later, in January 1982, Montana and Clark combined for the most famous play in 49ers history. It happened in one of those tough, grinding playoff games against the Dallas Cowboys. The 49ers trailed, 27–21, with time for one more possession. The winner of this bruising NFC title game would head for Super Bowl XVI. The loser would head home, grumbling about what might have been.

Dallas had been favored, with a cast of veterans and a great back in Tony Dorsett.

Walsh, however, unexpectedly gave the Cowboys a heavy dose of running on the 49ers' final possession, using veteran Lenvil Elliott in a lead role. With less than five minutes to play, Dallas expected Montana to throw on every down; the 49ers had finished nineteenth in rushing that year, averaging only 3.5 yards per carry, a league low. So the Cowboys set up to counter with a prevent defense, using two extra defensive backs and a three-man pass rush. The tactic played right into Walsh's strategy of using Elliott on power runs and Freddie Solomon on reverses.

With only 1:15 left on the clock, the 49ers were at the Dallas 13 yard line. After Montana missed Solomon in the end zone, Elliott gained seven yards on second down. Following a timeout, Walsh sent in a pass play known as the "sprint right option." Solomon ran an outside pattern on which Clark was supposed to screen, or pick, his defender.

"Dallas had it well scouted,' said Walsh. "They knew what we were about to do from the formation, so they just covered Freddie immediately."

As an option, Clark was supposed to run to the rear of the end zone and break towards the right sideline. Meanwhile, Montana was forced out of the pocket and began scrambling with 6-foot-9 Ed "Too Tall" Jones in close pursuit.

Clark was supposed to hook back if Solomon wasn't open. Sometimes quarterbacks and receivers think alike, and this was one of those times. Montana, chased to the sideline by Jones and two other Cowboys, saw Clark turn and slide towards the rear of the end zone. The ball left Montana's hands just before he stepped out of bounds. Clark, at 6-foot-4, went over rookie defender Everson Walls for the catch, timing his leap like a basketball rebounder. Montana's pass appeared too high for anyone but a seven-footer.

"Joe made a miraculous play out of it," said Walsh. "There were three guys chasing him down, and he was still concentrating up the field. I mean, he was the greatest competitor I've ever seen."

There are skeptics who insist to this day that Montana's pass was a throwaway. A lot of them live in the Dallas-Fort Worth area. One of them is named Too-Tall Jones, who had been one of the frantic pursuers grasping for any part of Montana.

"It wasn't a well-executed play," said Walsh. "They helped us up front with their defensive line and their blitzes. When Freddie was covered, Joe had to hold the ball an extra second and a half before he threw it. But gee, what a miraculous play."

So miraculous that the play became known as "The Catch" in NFL lore. It also made Dwight Clark, the two hundred forty-ninth player taken in the Montana draft, very famous.

Carmen Policy, the 49ers' vice-president at the time, was sitting in the press box for "The Catch." At first he thought Montana was trying to throw the ball away. Then Clark made his amazing reception. Nearby, a woman who worked the 49ers' charter flights popped a bottle of champagne. Policy, realizing the Cowboys still had one more possession, told the woman to put the cork back in the bottle. "Get that bottle out of here!" he screamed. "This game isn't over until there's zero-zero-zero on the clock!" The woman started crying as the Cowboys went on offense—but after a game-saving tackle by Eric Wright and a fumble recovery by Jim Stuckey, she stopped.

Moments after Clark's soaring catch advanced the 49ers to their first Super Bowl, Bill Walsh knew he would be coaching for more than just a championship ring. This Super Bowl would be a game for everything he stood for and everything he believed in: His opponent would be the high-scoring Cincinnati Bengals, and Paul Brown, the team's legendary coach and general manager, had virtually blackballed Walsh from getting a head coaching job six years earlier.

***

When Brown retired as coach after the 1978 season, it was assumed that Walsh, the Bengals' offensive coordinator, would replace him. Instead, Brown had named Bill "Tiger" Johnson, his offensive line coach.

"It killed me," said Walsh. "It didn't kill me that Bill got the job, because he was a close friend. But it uprooted my life because if I had been passed over and stayed there; my chances of getting a head job were really slim. Paul felt it was all one big family, so why would anybody want to leave the family?"

It wasn't that Brown didn't consider Walsh tough enough to handle a team. That was just media talk in the press box. Actually, Brown felt that Walsh couldn't handle "the emotional highs and lows of the game," as fellow coach Dick Vermeil said.

There were seven other head coaching jobs open that year in Houston, New Orleans, Philadelphia, San Francisco, Seattle, Tampa Bay, and the New York Jets. The Seahawks and Bucs were expansion teams. The Jets, Oilers, Saints, and 49ers fired their coaches because they couldn't score. Yet, Walsh, the perfect choice to solve anybody's punchless offense, was passed over. Brown had put out the word, and his word was accepted as if it came from a pulpit.

At Cincinnati, Walsh had taught and polished Ken Anderson, a quarterback out of tiny Augustana College. Walsh remembered trying to take films of Anderson as a senior. "The camera was at the top of their bleachers, which was about the tenth row in," he said. "Every time Ken did something, everybody stood up and you couldn't see anything. I knew this. He could throw, and he was the biggest man on the field except for the tuba player." Anderson quickly fit into Walsh's offense with the Bengals. Ten years later, they would meet again, this time as adversaries in Super Bowl XVI.

Anderson led the league in passing that 1981 season: 3,754 yards with a 62.6 completion percentage; only one interception for every 48 passes. Walsh, his old mentor, meanwhile had swept all of the coach-of-the-year awards. Now in his third year with the 49ers, he'd turned a bickering 2–14 team into a precise, high-speed Super Bowl machine.

The 49ers were a young team then, presumably too young to win a Super Bowl except in their own dreams. Only two 49ers, middle line-backer Jack Reynolds and tight end Charle Young, had ever been in a Super Bowl, both in Super Bowl XIV with the Los Angeles Rams. Twenty-five players on the 49ers' 45-man roster had three years of experience or less. Eleven of them were rookies from Walsh's great 1981 draft.

The critics looked at Anderson and then looked at the San Francisco secondary. The 49ers' youthful unit (average age: 23 years, eight months) included three rookies: Ronnie Lott, Eric Wright, and Carlton Williamson. The veteran of the group was Dwight Hicks, a castoff who had been cut by two NFL teams, as well as the Toronto Argonauts, a Canadian Football League team. Yet Carmen Policy sensed that this secondary was a lot better than the unit that critics had pounced on. "Dwight Hicks had a certain smooth, refined value, patina, if you will, that he was able to administer to the secondary," said Policy. "That unit, combined with some of the elements that Bill added to the rest of the defense . . . everything just mixed well."

The pregame buzz should have been about Anderson and how he learned the tricks of the trade from Walsh, the teacher-pupil matchup and an old angle that sports editors always love. This was Anderson's eleventh year. He had matured into a star under Walsh's skillful coaching during his time with the Bengals. There was the fast drop back. The quick reads. The pocket instincts to escape trouble. He was Walsh's kind of quarterback.

The Bengals also had a mammoth fullback named Pete Johnson, who could get a tough yard anytime by "moving the pile," as the coaches say. One of his favorite plays was "36-M lead," a basic strong-side power play included in everyone's playbook. Johnson would follow a lead blocker over right tackle Mike Wilson, meaning over 500 pounds of muscle, churning legs, and body, slamming into the off-tackle hole.

There were other weapons that concerned the San Francisco defense. Halfback Charles Alexander had a burst of speed as did backup Archie Griffin. There were a trio of able receivers: tight end Dan Ross and wideouts Isaac Curtis and Cris Collinsworth, the latter a 6-foot-5 rookie who had caught 67 passes.

"We had a pretty good mix," said offensive coordinator Lindy Infante. "That's why we were a pretty solid football team."

Yet, the weather trumped every conceivable Super Bowl angle. The NFL owners had voted to play their first cold-weather Super Bowl in Pontiac, Michigan, a Detroit suburb. During the week, wind-whipped snow and ice storms gripped the city. By Sunday, the temperature had plunged to 26 degrees below zero.

Walsh got to the team hotel before his players, after arriving from a coach-of-the-year banquet in Washington, DC. Sensing that his young 49ers needed a laugh after their five-hour flight from California, Walsh borrowed a bellhop uniform to greet the team.

"I was nervous about doing it," said Walsh, "but I thought, why not? So I got a dark-reddish outfit that seemed like it hadn't been cleaned for a long time. I walked out when the buses pulled up. I put on dark glasses and pulled the hat low."

Most of the 49ers brushed past their coach. But Walsh managed to grab a bag from one of the players. When he reached for a tip, none was given.

"They didn't recognize me for a couple of minutes," Walsh said. "I just kept making trouble. I kept grabbing bags from the most defiant guys and trying to pull them away. I went with two or three guys that way. They caught on to it. Everybody had a good laugh. But I could have made a fool of myself. What if we had lost that game? I'd have been a clown."

But Bill Walsh wasn't finished with his tricks. The Bengals were out there complaining that they had to practice at the indoor Silverdome in suburban Pontiac. It was a tight fit because of a parade of rehearsals for the colorful pregame and halftime shows that featured pop star Diana Ross singing the national anthem.

A coin flip was used to decide the order of practice. The Bengals won the toss and chose to practice in the afternoon. The 49ers got the early workout, meaning they also had the early media session that started at 8:00 a.m.

"That was five in the morning our time," said Walsh. "And we had to have breakfast, get taped, and get our uniforms on. So we had to get up at 3:00 a.m. in the morning, our time. That was absurd. The Bengals, they were out there on their own time. It was hard for our guys to sleep. We were operating on nerve."

Walsh's daily gripe sessions weren't as biting as Bud Grant's before Super Bowl VIII, or George Allen's at Super Bowl VII. Grant, the Minnesota coach, had grumped about finding a sparrow in the shower room of a suburban Houston high school where the Vikings trained. Allen, who coached the Washington Redskins, complained about everything from the angle of the sun at the Los Angeles Coliseum to time-consuming sessions with the media and the presence of strange, attractive women in the lobby of the Redskins' hotel. Rather Walsh, in his complaints, was simply playing a role: Professor of Psychology. The title of his lecture: "The World Is against Us." Yet, nothing that happened during the hectic week would unnerve Walsh as much as the wild and wacky trip to the Silverdome on game day.

The 49ers team buses, already slowed by slick roads, came to a complete stop more than a mile from the stadium. The stall was caused by the arrival of Vice President George H.W. Bush's entourage, whose 16-car motorcade snarled traffic all around the stadium. According to Don Weiss, the NFL's Super Bowl director, Bush's aides had been warned about a potential traffic disaster. They were asked to arrive very early or just before the 4:00 p.m. kickoff. They did neither.

"If hell does freeze over, I can tell you what it might look like," fumed Weiss in his book, *The Making of the Super Bowl: The Inside Story of the World's Greatest Sporting Event.*

Many cars stalled along M-39, the only major feeder road to the stadium off Interstate 75. Other drivers parked their cars along the highways or side streets and plodded through snow-covered fields. Walsh was struck by the same idea as he sat in the stalled team bus.

"I could see the top of the dome," he said. "I looked around at the nearby hills and saw this cow path. Then I thought I'd lead the team over the cow path and down to the stadium that looked about a mile, two miles away."

Linebacker Keena Turner was on a team bus that stopped on the off-ramp from I-75. "What do you do, you're stuck," he said. "We were kind of at the mercy of the circumstances. But everybody was pretty lighthearted about it. Obviously, it didn't get in the way of our performance."

Some frantic sportswriters, fearing they might miss the opening kickoff, fled the crawling media buses and joined an army of fans trudging to the Silverdome. A few of them, knowing it would be 72 degrees inside the domed stadium, had left their coats at the hotel. They made it just in time to the media check-in, cursing all the way.

Walsh eventually decided against leading his team through the snow. Instead, he began spinning a few jokes to keep his players loose. "I said, 'Hey, they've kicked off and we're ahead, 3–0,' then I named some of our equipment men who were playing for us. I got a little laugh out of it, but I'm sure it was just out of me and four or five players. Thank God for Joe Montana."

Walsh gave his team a brief pep talk before the game.

"The Bengals aren't going to take this game away from us," Walsh told his players. "We deserve it. We're here, and it's for us to take because we're the best team in the world."

The teams barely had enough time to dress, tape, and conduct their personal pre-game routines. The 49ers had dominated the Bengals, 21–3, in the regular season, forcing six turnovers (three interceptions, three fumble recoveries). Yet, the Bengals were installed as a one-point betting favorite, based on MVP quarterback Ken Anderson, their overall experience, and a starting lineup that included eight No. 1 draft picks. "Probably the best personnel in the league," said Walsh.

Walsh, however, was up to his usual game-day tricks. He sometimes used an unbalanced line, flopping tackles Dan Audick or Keith Fahnhorst to the other side. Surprisingly, the 49ers rushed for 127 yards with their anonymous backfield of Earl Cooper and Ricky Patton. Defensive end Fred Dean turned up everywhere, sometimes as a blitzing linebacker. "He was awfully quick, and Kenny sometimes had to hold the ball," said Jim McNally, the Bengals' offensive line coach. "Fred Dean was a problem."

When the 49ers had played Detroit in the season opener at the Silverdome, Walsh had noticed how the kickoffs sometimes took crazy bounces on the synthetic AstroTurf. So, in the Super Bowl, Walsh ordered Ray Wersching, his veteran kicker, to "squib" his kickoffs, sending them bounding downfield. Returner Archie Griffin fumbled one of them just five seconds before halftime, and the resulting turnover gave the 49ers an easy field goal, one of four that Wersching would kick.

"They surprised us in the first half by squib-kicking a couple of times," said Bengals coach Forrest Gregg in a press conference after the Super Bowl. "The ball was really hard to handle in that dome. Being as cold as it was outside and heated inside, it dried up the AstroTurf, and the ball just kind of went crazy."

Walsh also gave the Bengals the fake reverse, the real reverse, and a 14-yard pass to Charle Young off a triple reverse. He gave them Ricky Patton on outside runs off the unbalanced line. He gave them a heavy dose of Montana's passes (10 of Walsh's first 15 calls were passes). And he gave them something called the "Fox Two Special."

Early in the second quarter, following a fumble recovery, Walsh called for the Fox Two Special, a play he hadn't used since training camp. On that play, receivers Dwight Clark and Freddie Solomon lined up on the same side, both to run inside routes. Clark and Solomon made their cuts, clearing out the left side. Cooper faked a fullback dive, swung into the clearing, and gathered Montana's first-down pass for an 11-yard touchdown. That score gave the 49ers a 14–0 lead.

By halftime, Montana had taken the 49ers on three long scoring drives of 68, 92, and 61 yards. Walsh next called for an even mix to keep the Bengals defense off-balance: 19 runs, 19 passes. When Wersching made a last-second field goal off the bobbled kick by Griffin, the 49ers had opened a 20–0 halftime lead.

"That season, he was the difference-maker," Walsh would say of Wersching. "His medium and short field goals were virtually 100 percent. He was different, from the old country. Maybe Bosnia or Croatia, some country like that. [It was actually Mondsee, Austria]. He was fun, but he had nerves of steel kicking the ball."

Walsh knew the Bengals weren't beaten yet—and he knew because he had coached Ken Anderson and studied him on tape long into the night. Chuck Studley, Walsh's defensive coordinator, elected to play a soft zone going into the second half. The logical idea was to prevent the big play, the long strike to Collinsworth or Ross or Curtis that could swing the momentum and still leave enough time for Anderson to work his magic on the young 49ers secondary.

"I told them at halftime that I wasn't comfortable with the lead," said Walsh. "I told them what to expect. We were playing a great team. Maybe if it had been 24–0 the Bengals might have caved in, but not with the score 20–0."

As Walsh predicted, the Bengals scored on the first possession of the third quarter. And with Anderson finding his rhythm, they drove to a first down at the 49ers' 3 yard line later in the period. The 49ers, however, made one of the greatest goal-line stands in Super Bowl history to halt the drive at the 1 yard line. The 49ers' run-stoppers twice stopped Johnson. Then Anderson swung a little flat pass to Alexander. Linebacker Dan Bunz delivered a quick, waist-high tackle and threw Alexander back before he could break the plane of the goal line. "Dan had to make a perfect tackle in the open field," said Studley. "Here's a guy [Alexander] who weighs 220 pounds and can run and has only a yard to go to score."

On fourth down, the Bengals ran Johnson again on their pet 46 M lead play. But Hacksaw Reynolds led a wave of defenders to plug the hole and keep the Bengals inches from the end zone.

"I think they anticipated, yeah," said Gregg. "They closed the gaps. The middle linebacker [Reynolds] did a good job anticipating. Getting him was the key. Everybody else was locked up man for man. We just didn't have people to account for him. It was the first time all season that we were stopped on that play."

"If I had it to do all over again, I'd still give it to Pete," said offensive coordinator Lindy Infante. "The feeling was to give it to the big back. Golly, if we can't get a yard, we probably don't deserve to win the game anyway."

The Bengals scored early in the fourth period on Anderson's 4-yarder to Ross, cutting the 49ers' lead to 20–14. But Wersching hit his fourth field goal on the next series, and the 49ers held on to win their first Super Bowl, 26–21.

"There was no pressure on them really to score," said Gregg. "It was on us to score quickly. If we had made the touchdown [on Johnson's plunge], personally I think it could have been a different ballgame."

Gregg was right. The 49ers ran on 19 of their last 24 plays in the second half, nursing the lead and the clock. Even after the Bengals scored twice to trail just 20–14, the 49ers ran Cooper eight times on two time-consuming drives that ended with field goals by Wersching.

Clark, the towering receiver, cradled an onsides kick with 16 seconds left that "scared" Walsh as it bounded upfield. Montana then dropped to a knee, running out the clock and giving the 49ers their first Super Bowl championship. It was a victory for the organization, the city—and Bill Walsh's unique "boxing theory."

On both of the key goal-line tackles, Bunz and Reynolds quickly reacted to the flow of the play, like boxers picking off a blow in mid-air. That's how it's done on *defense*. On *offense*, Walsh taught it the other

Bill Walsh celebrates a win in Super Bowl XVI in 1982, the team's first championship.

way around, the "boxer" exploding with his punch before the defender can react.

The 49ers, 17 of whom had suffered with Walsh through a dreadful 2–14 season in 1979, danced off the field as if it was their personal red carpet and this was their Oscar night. Several of them hoisted Walsh to their shoulders.

"It was just euphoric," said Walsh. "You're still in some sort of quasi-mindset. That whole experience, you're sort of operating on nerve. It was surreal, I guess the word would be. Then suddenly you're on your players' shoulders while the whole place is alive."

There was virtual pandemonium in the locker room. Eddie DeBartolo Jr. was there with dozens of his friends from Youngstown, Ohio, where the DeBartolo Corporation was located, as was Eddie's father.

"My guess is that Eddie had over 100 people at that game," said Walsh. "It was such an incredible thing. Eddie DeBartolo Sr. was so proud of the team and what it had done. He had never seen so many people excited and satisfied. And, of course, I felt the same way."

Later, when the revelry shifted to the 49ers' hotel, Bill and Geri Walsh and two other friendly couples were blocked from getting to the team party. There were hundreds of fans and curiosity seekers who virtually bottlenecked the hotel entrance. Walsh tried several side entrances, but found the doors locked.

"It was 20 degrees outside, and we couldn't get back into the hotel," said Walsh. "We were stuck out there, pounding on the wall. We were out there for 10 or 15 minutes before we got to the party."

Walsh spotted Eddie DeBartolo, grinning and acting like a king. And why not? "Fantastic," DeBartolo told his coach.

Dianne Feinstein, then the new mayor of San Francisco, decided that the city should honor its new heroes with a Super Bowl parade. Walsh was against the idea, but mayors always trump coaches when it comes to celebrations.

"I didn't know who would come," the mayor said. "But when we headed up Market Street, there were people hanging from the lamp posts to see us. All of a sudden, hope and promise came to a city that had lived in the dark for a couple of years. People were a bit nicer; antagonism seemed less . . . . The Niners were part of critical history."

DeBartolo and the other 49ers management officials rode in open limousines. The coaches and players climbed aboard motorized cable cars for the occasion.

"I did not think anyone would bother to turn out during the day for a football team driving down the street," said Walsh. "I just didn't think that was possible. And when we got off the plane after winning the Super Bowl, they put us on these trolleys on wheels, and we turned the corner and started down the Embarcadero. There were just a handful of people on a corner and a handful on the next corner. And I thought, *God, is this going to be embarrassing. Going down Market Street, stalling traffic. No one's going to be there.* Well, we turned a corner and it was *unbelievable.* I don't know if there have ever been more people at one singular so-called parade, or celebration, anywhere at any time. It was huge. Hanging from windows, or light posts, just thousands upon thousands of people, a hundred deep. It was mind-boggling. The noise and the excitement were unbelievable.

"And when we turned that corner and I looked in these people's eyes. I saw young people, tall people, short people, people of color, Asian people, much older people. I saw a cross-section of people, all standing in unison . . . from the top executives down to the people who clean the streets, right next to each other, screaming. It was just the most electrifying moment I've ever had.

"I think the 49ers brought the city together. It became San Francisco again. The city became a World's Champion for the first time, and all those kinds of things [differences] were forgotten. And minimized because we had turned an entire state around. And a huge and great city around because of professional football. We had more of an impact than you would ever think. On our young, on our old, and the way people feel about themselves, others, and the city."

Carmen Policy felt the 49ers' style of play had something to do with the huge number of fans turning out for the parade. "You have to do things with pizzazz here," he said. "The West Coast offense has flair and finesse. There is a certain connection to execution. This team transcended typical brute strength. And I think people reveled in that. It was like watching the diminutive karate champion beat the heavyweight."

Keena Turner was thrilled by the noise and the size of the crowd.

"It was special to come back like that," he said. "It felt like the whole city was out. Confetti and appreciation everywhere we went."

Brent Jones, the tight end, called the celebration "an absolute love fest. The city was just lined with people. It gave us a wonderful, wonderful feeling. The city seemed so to be so involved and so engaged with the team and wanted to share the moment. People in the Bay Area lived and breathed 49er football. I mean, people were *obsessed*. People talked about it at work. It was on the radio stations, it was in the shopping centers. It was 49ers all the time."

Eddie DeBartolo Jr., the driving owner, had given the 49ers the stage, lavish and costly. Bill Walsh, the brilliant head coach, had given his struggling team the system and the players to fit it. On this very special day of joy and memories, with the sun sparkling off the bay, they were the Kings of San Francisco.

CHAPTER 7

SUPER AGAIN AND AGAIN

THE PROBLEMS THAT stopped the 49ers the next year, 1982, had nothing to do with execution on the field. Suddenly there was a drug problem. Then a 57-day player strike that cut the season to nine games. The 49ers finished with a 3–6 record, losing six games by a total of 27 points.

Walsh had hired Dr. Harry Edwards to prepare psychological tests for potential draft choices and to counsel young players. Walsh suspected his team included several drug users, but he would not confirm that to reporters.

Beneath the surface, there was also a private dispute with Montana, with Walsh claiming his system had made his quarterback a superstar, and Montana insisting it was the other way around. Walsh was also critical of Montana's off-day television appearances. "It's taking away from his concentration," said Walsh. "I'm really concerned that a potentially great career is going to dwindle away." Montana quit his television show after the first year, but it was his inability to maintain his charisma in front of the camera rather than Walsh's prodding that made him leave.

The 49ers rebounded from their drab record in 1982 to win their division the following year, routing Dallas, 42–17, on the final day of the season. Walsh had made four coaching changes, the most notable involving Chuck Studley, his defensive coordinator. For several years Walsh had wanted a more innovative defensive scheme. To accomplish that, he elevated George Seifert to design a new situation system based on down-and-distance. It was the hot defensive topic in the '80s, when teams had begun to open up their offenses and using the shotgun formation on passing downs.

In their 1983 NFC title game, the 49ers trailed Washington, 21–0, but staged a fourth-quarter rally as Montana threw three touchdown passes. Then it all slipped away, as the Redskins kicked a last-second field goal.

Walsh and DeBartolo were furious at two critical calls that helped sink the 49ers. In the first, Eric Wright had been called for pass interference on an overthrown ball. "I pushed him, but it was after the ball was away overthrown," said Wright. Walsh said the pass "could not have been caught by a 10-foot Boston Celtic." Later on the same drive, Ronnie Lott was flagged on a holding call as a Redskins pass fell incomplete.

The next season, the resolute 49ers would not be denied their second Super Bowl title. The 1983 draft had produced three future starters: halfback Roger Craig, linebacker Rikki Ellison, and center Jesse Sapolu, an eleventh round pick. Wendell Tyler rushed for 1,262 yards. Montana had another brilliant season, passing for 3,630 yards and 28 touchdowns as the 49ers finished with a 15–1 record. Their only loss was a 20–17 squeaker to the Pittsburgh Steelers.

The pregame hype to Super Bowl XIX was all about Dan Marino, Miami's second-year quarterback, who had thrown for NFL records of 5,048 yards and 48 touchdown passes, most of them to Mark Duper and Mark Clayton. The Marino hype finally got to Montana.

"You don't mind being overlooked that much, but sometimes it seemed they [reporters] forgot there were two teams in the game," said Montana. "It got to all of us after a while. But you couldn't argue with Dan's statistics. He had a great season."

As the game progressed, it became obvious that the 49ers were far more balanced than the pass-minded Dolphins. Montana not only passed for 331 yards and three touchdowns, he also eluded the Dolphin rush to scramble for 59 yards. Craig gave the 49ers the best game of his career: 58 rushing yards, eight catches for 82 yards, and three touchdowns.

The lightweight Miami linebackers simply couldn't match up to Walsh's offense. In one crazy sequence, Montana scrambled down the sideline behind a Dolphins linebacker who was chasing Craig.

"We looked at some films and we said, 'This is a Super Bowl defense?'" said Walsh. "It's unusual for a one-dimensional team to make it to the Super Bowl. We could see in the films that we could run against them."

The 49ers also felt that Miami's defensive scheme for short passes, designed by former 49ers coach Chuck Studley, could be easily exploited. Studley's plan was to give the 49ers the short pass and protect against the deep throw. Walsh had the perfect answer with Montana's quick, effective passes.

"Bill had his game plan in surprisingly early," said receiver Dwight Clark. "We just had a lot of time to perfect it. Everything that was open on film was open in the game. Especially 'out' patterns and stuff underneath for the backs."

Marino, who had broken all those league passing records, finished with one touchdown pass, a little 2-yarder to Dan Johnson. It gave Miami a brief lead before Montana and the 49ers scored 21 straight points to take over the game. Marino, who had averaged 9.1 yards a pass play during the season, averaged only 5.4 yards in his first Super Bowl. Of Marino's record 50 passes, 19 were thrown into the short zones; only 13 into the deep zones. He completed only three long passes, none for more than 30 yards.

The obvious tactic against a pass-rushing line is to run the ball inside the looping ends and to scramble. When the Dolphins ran, they found the lanes jammed. And the 49ers knew that Marino was one of the worst scramblers in the league.

The Dolphins ranked sixteenth in rushing, and they looked worse in this Super Bowl. Halfback Tony Nathan averaged 3.6 yards on five carries, fullback Woody Bennett 2.3 yards on three. The Dolphins appeared to give up too early on their running game after twice running into defensive end Fred Dean.

"I think some people underrated our defense," said Walsh, who won a fascinating tactical game with Dolphins coach Don Shula. "Everybody talked about the Chicago Bears, but we are possibly the strongest defense in pro football. Basically, we went after them with everything we had. And I think we proved that a diversified offense that can move the ball on the ground, as well as in the air, might be more effective than an offense that leans on the pass."

Walsh threw a variety of play-action and misdirection gambits at Shula's defense. On a typical Walsh pass play, Montana faked to fullback Roger Craig who swept behind pulling guard Randy Cross, then threw to tight end Russ Francis for 19 yards. Reflecting on Montana's ability to find open receivers, the game's Most Valuable Player was 13-for-18 for 102 yards on short passes, 9-for-11 for 163 yards on medium passes and 2-for-6 for 66 yards on long passes.

"We just couldn't put two good defensive plays in a row," said Miami defensive end Doug Betters. "They made it on second-and-long, third-and-long, and Montana was responsible for a lot of that. They just drilled us."

Sure, Marino had receivers open on almost every pass play. But most of them were in the shallow zones and the 49ers gambled—correctly, as it turned out—that Marino's short game wasn't going to beat them. The 49ers simply had too much defensive firepower and too much of an offensive mix for a Dolphins defense that always seemed to be a step short and sometimes two steps late.

Walsh's offensive game plan, of course, had a lot to do with that. So did Montana's daring scrambles that produced 59 yards, more than twice the Dolphins' rushing total. On four of the five series that Montana scrambled, the 49ers scored three touchdowns and a field goal.

"Going in, we told him to take what you see," said Walsh. "He was able to evade their pass rushers, not the fastest in the league, so he ran and ran very successfully."

At one point, after Craig turned a short dump pass into a 16-yard touchdown and a 38–16 lead, Shula approached his defensive coordinator on the Miami sideline. Studley responded by throwing up his hands in apparent disgust.

Like Walsh, Shula had his own bag of tactics. Early in the game, when the Dolphins had receivers open and appeared to be competitive, Marino worked without a huddle from the shotgun. But, on defense, the Dolphins had to play it straight from their 3-4 alignment without A. J. Duhe, their ailing linebacker.

"We needed turnovers, and we didn't get them," said linebacker Bob Brudzinski. "They are a helluva team. You can't complain about losing a game like this."

The Dolphins were also hurt by Reggie Roby's a mediocre performance. Roby normally delivered towering punts with five-second hang time. In the Super Bowl, he got off a series of weak punts of 37, 40, and 39 yards in the first half. He regained his form in the second half, but it was too late.

Roby's performance had company. The Miami defense kept missing tackles and never could get to Montana (they were credited with one sack when Montana slipped). The Dolphins' offensive line, which had allowed only 14 sacks in the regular season and none in the playoffs, had all it could handle, particularly after the 49ers took the lead and Dean, Dwaine Board, and Gary Johnson cut loose.

"We knew they couldn't run," said 49ers defensive line coach Bill McPherson. "So we used a lot of different line calls. We did a lot of stunting. We used a lot of calls against them, eight different ones I think, and we used five or six guys. Outside, Dwaine Board had a helluva game. And inside, Gary Johnson was a force. He's the strongest guy in the weight room. And he's quick off the ball. One step and he's gone."

The San Francisco defense sacked Marino four times, overpowering the Dolphins inside, led by defensive tackle Gary "Big Hands" Johnson, and using some of Seifert's new line stunts. In another of those amazing deals that Walsh kept pulling off, the 49ers had acquired Johnson from San Diego. The Chargers had tried to play Johnson outside, a failed experiment. Marino ended up throwing 50 passes, while the Dolphins ran only nine times, the most lopsided pass-run ratio in Super Bowl history.

When it was all over, as the 49ers were celebrating their 38–16 romp in front of the cameras, losing coach Don Shula conceded the obvious.

"Offensively, it was our poorest game of the year," he said. "We were stopped today."

"He [Marino] didn't have time to look off his receivers," said 49ers free safety Dwight Hicks. "He was getting too much pressure from our line. We weren't going to get beat with short passes." Safety Carlton Williamson said the 49ers, usually a zone team, played more man-to-man coverage, backing the corners eight yards off the ball. Marino's longest completion was a 30-yarder to backup tight end Joe Rose.

Yet, it was the 49ers' front four of Lawrence Pillers, Manu Tuiasosopo, Dwaine Board, and Gary Johnson who all but took over the game.

"You could see him getting rattled out there," said Johnson. "Marino would throw away passes, or he would talk more than usual to his offensive linemen. We could see we were getting to him. But you'd be upset, too, if you were getting hit a lot."

Marino admitted the 49ers' changeup pass coverages were a lot stronger than he expected. "Sometimes I didn't throw the ball well," he said. "Sometimes I didn't have time, and sometimes the guys didn't get open." he said. "They played the best any team has played against us defensively. They took us out of our scheme."

In their earlier Super Bowl years, the Dolphins had been a formidable running team. These were the years of Larry Csonka, Jim Kiick, and a solid offensive line headed by Hall of Famer Larry Little. But Shula sensed that a series of major rules changes was designed to turn the NFL into a pass-and-catch league. Accordingly, Shula made Marino his pick in a historic 1983 draft that produced six first-round quarterbacks. After losing the Super Bowl in his second year, Marino felt sure he would get another chance, but never came close. Thus he joined a list of great quarterbacks who never won a diamond-studded Super Bowl ring, including Jim Kelly, Fran Tarkenton, Warren Moon, and Dan Fouts.

Montana would win two more rings before a serious back injury changed his career and brought Steve Young off the bench to run the highly successful West Coast offense. Walsh pulled off a major trade at the top of the 1985 draft, sending four choices to the New England Patriots and picking receiver Jerry Rice from Mississippi Valley State in the first round. Rice had caught 301 passes and scored 50 touchdowns for the Delta Devils, so he wasn't an unknown. Taking no chances, Walsh made one of the most historic draft-day deals for a player who set 18 Division 1-AA records in his college career. Montana and Rice quickly became the league's best pass-and-catch combination.

Four years later, in January 1989, the 49ers would put to rest rumors that they were aging and that Joe Montana had lost some off his magic. Their opponent in Super Bowl XXXIII was Cincinnati, coached by Sam Wyche, a former Walsh disciple. There was concern that the Super Bowl had also lost its edge. Too many blowouts. Too many inferior teams from the AFC, which had lost four straight Super Bowls by an average of 27.3 points.

But then Montana and the 49ers produced one of the most exciting of all Super Bowls against the nervy Bengals.

To add to the drama of the game, several key players knew of Walsh's impending retirement and that he was likely coaching his last game.

In Super Bowl XXIII, Rice frustrated the Bengals' secondary, catching 11 passes for 215 yards, often beating double coverage. The 49ers needed them all, especially the last one, a 27-yarder on second-and-20 that kept the 49ers' winning 92-yard drive going.

"We triple-teamed Rice," said Wyche. "Somehow, Joe got the ball to him." Cornerback Lewis Billups, one of the three defenders, described the play as "a perfect throw and catch." Two plays later, with only 34

Receiver Jerry Rice catches a touchdown pass in Super Bowl XXIII.

seconds to play, Montana threw the winning touchdown pass to John Taylor, using Rice as a decoy.

"The Super Bowl was finally super," gushed 49ers' center Randy Cross, who also retired after 13 seasons. "It was a game that you can look back on and say, 'Now *that* was a game.'"

It was Walsh's third Super Bowl championship, following wins in Super Bowl XVI (26–21 over Cincinnati), and Super Bowl XIX (38–16 over Miami). "But this team should stand on its own," Walsh was later to say. "They were not just one of the three teams that won. They battled long odds to do it. They are just as good as the others."

The 49ers had struggled most of the year with a quarterback controversy involving Montana and Steve Young. Rice had been hobbled by a severe ankle injury. But in the stretch run to the playoffs, Walsh went to Montana and Rice regained his health. The year's biggest hurdle before

Super Bowl XXIII had been the NFC title game played in Chicago with a minus-26 degrees wind-chill factor. Montana chilled the Bears with three touchdown passes, two to Rice, in a 28–3 victory.

Coming into the Super Bowl, the Bengals were hardly another AFC pushover. Wyche had fashioned an explosive offense built around Boomer Esiason's play-action passes, rookie fullback Ickey Woods' cutback runs behind a huge slanting line, and a no-huddle scheme. The Bengals' so-called "spinner defense"—defenders "spun" into different positions—employed as many as 23 different players.

The 49ers had taken the high road to the Super Bowl with a $15.1 million payroll, almost $2 million more than the Bengals' $13.4 million. The 49ers also outclassed the Bengals in facilities, scouting, and comfort travel. "What the hell," said 49ers owner Eddie DeBartolo Jr. "Maybe I want to do things out of the ordinary."

High road or low road, the 49ers and Bengals put on a spectacular show. The 49ers had no early rhythm. Mike Cofer missed a 19-yard field goal after a bad snap. Roger Craig lost a fumble.

The Bengals lost much more when Pro Bowl nose tackle Tim Krumrie broke the tibia and fibula in his lower left leg on the seventh defensive snap. Yet, the Bengals hung tough. Jim Breech kicked two field goals. Stanford Jennings, whose wife had given birth to a daughter the day before, sprinted up a middle lane to score on a 93-yard kickoff return. And when Breech kicked a 40-yard field goal, the Bengals led 16–13, with only 3:20 left to play.

That's when Joe Montana took over the game on a dramatic 11-play, 92-yard drive. The winning score was a 10-yard bullet to John Taylor, known in the playbook as 20 Halfback Curl X Up. Roger Craig was the primary receiver on a curl route, but he lined up in an incorrect spot. Taylor lined up in a tight end position, while Rice went in motion, right to left, and broke outside as a decoy, drawing the Bengals to the strong side of the field. Taylor then beat nickelback Ray Horton inside for Montana's game-winner.

"The drive was extremely well-executed," said Walsh. "We had a long way to go, but Joe handled the no-huddle beautifully, and Jerry Rice was a great vehicle that we had."

Before the 49ers' winning drive, an overexcited teammate came up to Bengals' receiver Cris Collinsworth and gushed, "Well, we got 'em now." *Sports Illustrated's* Paul Zimmerman related that Collinsworth replied, "Have you seen who is quarterbacking the 49ers? Joe Montana is not human. I don't want to call him a god, but he's somewhere in-between."

Moments after the game ended, Walsh was overcome with emotion. Confetti was in the air, there were flashing lights, and a mass of players, officials, and reporters jammed the field. He found Wyche approaching from the opposite side.

"The moment had gotten to all of us," said Wyche. "It was his last game. We hugged. He told me, 'I love you'. . . . and I replied, 'I love you, too.'"

It was a moment of high drama. "We put our arms around each other," said Wyche. "Then he tripped and I grabbed him. He didn't come right back up. I just wanted to make sure he didn't go to the ground. I told him, 'Great game . . . you deserved it.'"

There existed one play that would have given the Super Bowl trophy to Wyche and the Bengals. Billups muffed a chance to intercept a Montana pass in the end zone just before the game-winner to Taylor. The ball bounced around like a windblown balloon and fell to the ground. "If we just make that catch . . . ," Wyche was saying when asked about the play 30 years after it happened. "There were 50 or 55 seconds to play and they had only one timeout left." It's an agonizing thought that will never leave his mind.

In 1986, John Taylor had been the 49ers' third-round pick in another of Walsh's productive drafts that also produced fullback Tom Rathman, corners Tim McKyer and Don Griffin, defensive end Charles Haley, offensive tackle Steve Wallace, and defensive tackle Kevin Fagan. In 1988 he had survived a month-long four-game suspension for failing a second pre-season drug test. "I worked out hard through it all," he said. With the Bengals keying on Rice and Craig, nobody jammed Taylor coming off the line. He gave a little head fake outside, cut back inside, and was wide open. "I split the defense," said Taylor. "When I turned around, I didn't see anyone."

After spiking the ball, Taylor looked at the clock that showed 34 seconds left to play. "The way the game was going, I knew we weren't safe until I saw double-zero," he said.

Taylor never received a college scholarship and ended up playing at Delaware State as a walk-on.

"I always thought I could play," he said. "I make the best of my situation and wait for my turn. Jerry [Rice] is a great receiver who is going to catch a lot more balls than me, and that is fine." Said receivers coach Dennis Green, "He [Taylor] has dedicated himself to football. He has become a big-play man."

CHAPTER 8
WALSH FEELS BURNED OUT

A **WEEK AFTER THEIR** thrilling Super Bowl XXIII victory, Bill Walsh and defensive coordinator George Seifert headed in different directions. Walsh and his wife, Geri, took a two-week vacation in Hawaii, to relax as the warm tropical breezes blew over them. Seifert headed for chilly Cleveland, where he was the unofficial favorite for the Browns' vacant head coaching job.

Walsh was weary from another season of 17-hour work days that extended into the night. His decision to retire from coaching, previously known only to a dozen veteran players, shocked the 49ers organization. Walsh left Eddie DeBartolo Jr. to contemplate a worthy successor: a coach who would continue to win more Super Bowls, a coach as innovative as Bill Walsh.

DeBartolo's choice was Jimmy Johnson, a highly successful college coach at the University of Miami. DeBartolo liked Johnson's fun-loving personality. He also liked his skill in evaluating players. University of Miami, which had won a national championship in 1987, had 55 of its players drafted in the first two rounds from 1985 to 1987, three of them first-rounders in 1987: quarterback Vinny Testaverde, halfback Alonzo Highsmith, and defensive tackle Jerome Brown. The college was virtually a feeder school for NFL players during the Johnson years.

Walsh told DeBartolo that Seifert should be his successor, keeping the same creative defensive scheme in place and the same West Coast system with Mike Holmgren, a brilliant offensive mind, as coordinator.

It was then Walsh caught the coaching fever again.

It was spring in San Francisco, time for the player draft and off-season workouts. But it was too late. DeBartolo, seeking continuity, had already settled on Seifert. Meanwhile, the 49ers began talking about a Super Bowl repeat. If any of the players needed any extra incentive, outspoken safety Ronnie Lott gave them a slogan that spread through the ranks: "We'll Show Walsh." The line was meant to convey that this was such a talented team that it could dominate the league once more, even without "The Genius." And when Seifert officially became Walsh's successor, no 49er was more thrilled than Lott. Yet, it remained for Seifert's wife, Linda, to supply the fitting line. "Don't screw it up, George," she told her husband.

Back in Cleveland, the Browns were left to think about what might have been. Seifert was headed for his interview with the Browns when Carmen Policy, now the 49ers' president, called him during a stopover in Dallas and told him to return to San Francisco because he was going to be named the 49ers' new head coach.

"I didn't want to lose George," said Walsh. "So Eddie, my attorney Steve Kay, Carmen Policy, and I met in Pebble Beach and discussed all this. We got George on the phone, and he flew back from Cleveland. There was all this talk about Jimmy Johnson. I think that would have been a mistake. Not that I didn't think Jimmy [wasn't] a good coach, but to change what we already had in place with a new coach and a new staff right at that juncture would have been a waste of a year or two."

Not long after Seifert had been named the new head coach, Walsh officially announced his retirement.

"I didn't mention anything about being tired or anything like that," he said. "I just said it was time to move on."

With his name and his Super Bowl success, Walsh was courted by NBC to appear as a studio analyst.

"It was all right," he was later to say. "If I had been a younger man who wanted to do television, that would have been an incredible opportunity for me. But for a middle-aged man like me, at my age, I didn't have that much feel for it."

Instead of analysis, NBC paired Walsh with Dick Enberg, its top sports announcer, to do color commentary.

"It was the No. 1 team," said Walsh. "I didn't even know there was a No. 1 team, or a No. 2." Walsh had signed a two-year contract that was extended for another two years. Walsh, however, decided to leave after his third year.

"You know how fickle that business is," he said. "I had been at a certain pace of doing things and having difficult responsibilities when I coached the 49ers. I never felt at the mercy and beck and call of someone else. Now, in network television, there are layers of people. There's the president, the GM, the news director, the sports director, and the production people. Any one of them could really cause trouble, and who needs that? I never felt uncomfortable, but I never felt that I came close to doing as well as I could, just by the nature of the way they did it."

***

Seifert took over a team gifted with talent: A star-packed offense, a tenacious defense, great depth, and the league's best quarterback. Holmgren had already proven that he was a terrific game-day coach. So it wasn't really surprising when the 49ers finished the 1989 season with a 14–2 record, losing only to the Los Angeles Rams by a point and Green Bay by four points. With Montana dominating the playoff games, the 49ers routed Minnesota, 41–13, and avenged their loss to the Rams, 30–3. As impressive as those games were, they were just jabs compared to the knockout punch thrown at Denver in Super Bowl XXIV.

When it was over, when the 49ers had routed the Broncos, 55–10, in the most lopsided of all Super Bowls, Seifert knew how it would all play out in the media and on the streets of San Francisco. Sure, the 49ers had won back-to-back Super Bowls, but these were Bill Walsh's

DeBartolo and Seifert after winning San Francisco's fourth Super Bowl.

players (17 of the 22 starters were holdovers from Walsh's last team), and it was Bill Walsh's creative offensive scheme.

"God would have had trouble beating them today," said Pat Bowlen, Denver's grim-faced owner. "In fact, they had God today." Bowlen, of course, meant Montana, who made the owner's Broncos look like a collection of castoffs and has-beens.

Montana completed 22 of 29 passes for 297 yards and a record five touchdowns. His totals in four Super Bowls were off the charts—83 completions in 122 attempts, 1,142 yards, 11 touchdowns, not a single interception. In 17 playoff games, 13 of which the 49ers won, Montana completed 335 of 538 pass attempts for 4,294 yards and 39 touchdowns.

"Our machine was running again," piped Bubba Paris, the 49ers' fun-loving offensive tackle. "This is the best team that's ever been assembled in football." On offense, an underrated offensive line, with Paris, Steve Wallace, Randy Cross, Bruce Collie, and Terry Tausch as protectors, gave

Montana four or five seconds to throw the ball. And on the Superdome's fast carpet, receivers Jerry Rice and John Taylor ran great inside routes. Montana also benefitted from the inside-outside running by Tom Rathman and Roger Craig, who constantly broke loose on sweeps.

"A couple of times, we felt, with their two-deep safeties, that we could use some motion and sneak something down the middle," said Montana. He did, finding Jerry Rice on a deep post pattern for a 38-yard touchdown just before halftime. Rice finished with seven catches for 148 yards and three touchdowns.

Denver's John Elway, on the other hand, had the worst playoff game of his career. He had problems completing the simplest of sideline patterns. Indeed, on a dreadful 10-for-26 day, Elway completed only one pass longer than 15 yards, and that was a little shovel pass that Bobby Humphrey turned into a 27-yard gain. Otherwise, Elway was scrambling for his life. With 9:28 left to play, Coach Dan Reeves finally replaced Elway with backup Gary Kubiak, who wore a flak jacket to protect cracked ribs.

If this had been a scrimmage, George Seifert would have called it off at halftime, because Joe Montana was hammering his defense. But this was the Super Bowl, and this was Denver's defense, bigger, stronger and tougher than its finesse unit from Super Bowls XXI and XXII.

Seifert's defense had a lot to do with Elway's misfortune. Charles Haley, changing sides as a speed rusher, and defensive end Kevin Fagan constantly put the heat on Elway. And the 49ers used some well-conceived schemes, sometimes dropping rushing end Pierce Holt into a shallow zone defense after a fake rush.

After two periods, the Broncos had these demoralizing offensive figures: five first downs, 88 total yards, and only nine minutes and five seconds of possession time. When it was finally over and the backups had more playing time than they ever imagined, the quarterbacks who took the final snaps were Gary Kubiak and Steve Young. Young and Kubiak mopping up in the Super Bowl? Who would have believed it?

Invariably, the 49ers' romp in Super Bowl XXIV began a new round of comparisons. Was Seifert's first team the best of them all? Or was Walsh's 1984 team that went 15–1, coming within one score of an unbeaten Super Bowl season, the best?

Pro Bowl linebacker Keena Turner was quick to decide.

"I guess I'll have to finally talk about it," he said, "We had unbelievable focus and talent on this [Super Bowl XXIV] team. I'd have to say this is the best one. The '81 team was young and naïve, a team that wanted some respect. The '84 club was more of a veteran team, with guys like [defensive end] Fred Dean and [linebacker] Hacksaw Reynolds. It was a confident team. The '88 team was on the ropes all the time, but it wouldn't fall. This team has been able to focus on the matter at hand. We could be down by 14 and still be determined to come back. I think the key thing that George [Seifert] did was to have our defensive line keep Elway moving, never let him have a chance to set up."

Walsh never bothered to attend the team party. He sat alongside DeBartolo in the owner's box and watched the 49ers romp. Seventeen of the 22 starters had started the previous year on his last Super Bowl team.

"I didn't go to the party," said Walsh. "There was a lot of melancholy for me. I was excited for the team, but I didn't necessarily belong. It was now Eddie's team and George's team, and I was no longer a part of it. Eddie had his Super Bowl, so I don't think he cared one way or another."

***

As the players soon discovered, George Seifert was a tough, focused head coach who ran a very tight ship. He suspended cornerback Tim McKyer for insubordination after an argument about playing time. Running backs Roger Craig and Tom Rathman were critical of Seifert's desire to spread the ball around more on offense. Another back, Terrence Flagler abruptly left practice because he felt he deserved more playing time.

"The players are a little more aggressive towards each other and the coaching staff this year, because Bill Walsh is gone," said linebacker Charles Haley in an interview with the *San Francisco Chronicle*. "I'm usually up and down as a lineman. Now I'm only playing down, even though I'm listed as a linebacker. I don't even know what my role is. When he [Walsh] was here, he kept everything, and I mean *everything*, under his grasp. But George has let personalities surface more, and it's all come out. There's been a lot of role changes for everyone. And now I don't even know what my role is here. Last year I played up as a linebacker. They don't want any one player being a great player and getting too much attention, even though it happens. They want you to fit into the system, the team."

Dallas general manager Tex Schramm emerged as one of Seifert's biggest boosters.

"Everybody in football, when you talk about the 49ers' success, always points to Joe Montana and Roger Craig and Jerry Rice, "said Schramm. "But their defense had as much to do with them winning all those Super Bowls."

Seifert and Walsh had one common trait: Both were focused on the game and the system and how to keep a team sharp and consistent. Yet there was a feeling around the league that the game was headed for an overhaul, with new rules favorable to the offense, and to most fans as well. But, for now, there were almost as many head coaches with defensive backgrounds (12) as those with offensive backgrounds (16).

"Whenever people say a defensive coach has no qualifications to be a head coach, I say, 'We spend our whole time analyzing offenses,'" said defensive line coach Bill McPherson. Yet, the question remained. Did Seifert have the temperament to be a head coach, a position he'd held only twice—once at tiny Westminster College and at Cornell in the Ivy League—since graduating from Utah in 1964?

There was no doubt about his intensity and ability to focus.

"George is always drawing up cards for practice, and he was running a little late one day," recalled McPherson. "We were out on the field already, and George was wearing [flip-flops] in his office, and he was in a hurry, so he tripped down the back stairway, rolled down the stairs, and fell into the wall. He's lucky he didn't kill himself. The dent is still there, it's officially known as 'Seifert Corner.'

"He came out to practice and didn't even show us the bump on his head until later. We had to tell him to shake his head because his eyes were stuck. George just gets into that little zone of his."

Seifert had been a popular choice with 49ers fans. He was a native San Franciscan. But Carmen Policy was among the critics who doubted that Seifert could handle the job because of his quiet nature. Now, Seifert had coached the league's best defensive unit and sent almost as many defensive players to the Pro Bowl (eight for 22 total years), as Walsh's highly publicized offense (nine for 21 years). Still, there was always a question about Seifert's ability to relate to players the way Bill Walsh had, with openness, quick decisions, and an occasional funny line or two.

"When I first joined the team," said defensive back Eric Davis, "I was like everyone else. When I looked at George, I'd see the stone-faced guy on TV who never smiled and never talked to anyone. He seemingly had no relationship with any of the players. He rode me so hard that it made me wonder if I had stolen money from him. I didn't like him at first, but he brought out in me what he was trying to bring out. And I earned my stripes."

Seifert's drab personality came up after Super Bowl XXIII, when DeBartolo and team president Policy were sorting out candidates to succeed Walsh. Both had obviously heard Rice's line: "I thought George was the most serious person I had ever met," said the greatest receiver in 49ers history. Policy was among the doubters who felt Seifert's intensity would hamper his ability to keep the 49ers atop the pro football world where Bill Walsh had placed them, though there was little doubt about his football knowledge.

"He's unbelievably bright," safety Tim McDonald said. "You blow a play in practice, and even though he's on the other side of the field, the next thing you know he's talking to your [position] coach. He didn't need an extra set of eyes and have to hear the call or see the formation, and he knew what happened."

Successful pro coaches are like that. In training camps and workouts, they seem to have an extra set of eyes, scanning where players don't expect them to scan, taking it all in for the post-practice meetings. In training camp one summer, Bill Walsh spotted a free agent back named Bill Ring from 25 yards away. Impressed, he told general manager John McVay to sign him.

Seifert's first Super Bowl win was followed by five highly successful seasons, three of which ended with jarring defeats in the NFC Championship Game. Two of the losses were to the Dallas Cowboys and Coach Jimmy Johnson, the man Eddie DeBartolo had wanted to hire as Walsh's replacement. The Cowboys won both Super Bowls, leaving DeBartolo to ponder what might have been if the 49ers had hired Johnson.

"People asked what was the secret to the '94 Super Bowl victory that the 49ers enjoyed, and it was very simple," said Policy. "George Seifert, Eddie DeBartolo, and I sat in this room back in January or February of '94. Eddie wrapped his arms around us and said, 'Gentlemen, whatever you need to win, I'm going to give you.' Then, as he left the room, he said, 'and if you don't win, good luck, see you elsewhere.'"

By then, 1994, the 49ers had grown older. The team and the city had been rocked by the most debatable trade in their history. Joe Montana, their hero of heroes, had been traded to Kansas City, leaving Steve Young to quarterback Bill Walsh's West Coast offense. The six Seifert drafts leading to his second Super Bowl in 1994 produced only three Pro Bowlers: halfback Ricky Watters, defensive end Dana Stubblefield, and safety Merton Hanks. There was change in the air.

CHAPTER 9

THE SEIFERT YEARS

THE 49ERS' FOURTH Super Bowl win, after the 1989 season, and the first after Bill Walsh had left the team seemed to disprove all the knocks against George Seifert, his successor: He was too quiet and had a drab personality. He had a fiery temper. He was not a year-around football coach. He was defensive-minded while Walsh's West Coast offense had been the heart of all those other Super Bowl wins.

"He isn't a recluse exactly, but he's different—the quietest coach I've ever known," said Paul Wiggin, Minnesota Vikings Director of Pro Personnel and a good friend. "Seifert is the antithesis of [former Atlanta coach] Jerry Glanville."

When Seifert had been Walsh's defensive coordinator, he'd lost his temper during halftime at a game in Chicago and kicked a chalkboard, breaking a toe. Admitted Seifert, "I'm more spontaneous. [Walsh] is more calculating."

One witness to Seifert's sideline antics said he resembled an angry bird of prey, as he sometimes roamed the sidelines without the earphones that Walsh, the play-caller, would never discard.

A San Francisco native, Seifert was the oldest of three sons of a Mission District teamster. He had left Northern California rarely, once to play linebacker and study zoology at Utah, once to coach at Cornell, and on short trips with the 49ers.

In the offseason, he could often be found aboard a fishing boat. Seifert preferred to fish alone. He made sure to carry a phone in his tackle box, not to check up on Joe Montana or any of his defensive coaches, but to stay in touch with his family.

"When the sun goes down in the bay, I always call my wife" he said. "I just tell her it's time to put the barbecue on.'" If he had an unproductive day on the boat, Seifert said, "We're ready for that, too. I just tell her, 'It's time to go get the hot dogs.'"

In *Sports Illustrated*, writer Michel Silver told of the time that Seifert was thrown from a 20-foot fishing boat and nearly suffered a serious injury. Seifert was fishing with companions Bruce Hulick and Ed Nessel when a huge wave crashed into the boat, throwing all three men into the chilly waters. The 4,000-pound boat landed bottom-up, above Seifert and he was sucked towards the ocean floor. Eventually he got to the surface and yelled over to his companions.

The trio then began swimming for the shore, about 200 yards away. Seifert, however, collided with a large striped bass that weighed an estimated 25 pounds.

"So I start swimming in with the fish," Seifert related. "But now the waves are pounding me. And I'm wearing these rain pants, and they start sliding down over my knees. So now I can't swim. It's the fish or me and I'm sinking. Finally I had to let the fish go so I could take off my rain pants and swim in. When we got to the shore, we looked like drowned rats."

In his early years as the 49ers' head coach, Seifert never was able to judge young talent with the magic that Walsh had brought to his drafts from 1979 to 1988, historic drafts like the one in 1979 that produced quarterback Joe Montana and receiver Dwight Clark.

"I live my life partly because of the way he [Walsh] molded me," said Montana. "He took a 189-pound, skinny-legged quarterback out of Western Pennsylvania and gave me the opportunity to continue to do something that I loved."

There was that 1980 draft that included three starters: running back Earl Cooper, defensive end Jim Stuckey, and linebacker Keena Turner, plus two other useful players, punter Jim Miller and linebacker Craig Puki. There was also the great 1981 draft that gave the 49ers three secondary starters, Ronnie Lott, Eric Wright, and Carlton Williamson, and in 1983, Walsh took running back Roger Craig, linebacker Riki Ellison and eleventh-rounder Jesse Sapolu, an underrated center-guard drive blocker who gave the 49ers 15 productive seasons. In the 1985 draft, Walsh shocked the league by trading four high picks so he could select wide receiver Jerry Rice, a future Hall of Famer. In fact the best draft of the Walsh years was the 1985 draft. In previous wheeler-dealer drafts, the 49ers had piled up three third-round picks and three fourth-rounders. Walsh hit on every one, getting running back Tom Rathman, corner Tim McKyer, and receiver John Taylor as third-rounders, and defensive end Charles Haley, offensive tackle Steve Wallace, and defensive tackle Kevin Fagan as fourth-rounders.

Said Walsh, "There aren't many great all-around players—any year—in the draft. So, at every position, we try to find players who offer something specific, who have an area of expertise that can be helpful to us."

From 1979 to 1988, Walsh drafted 29 starters. Among them were 12 Pro Bowlers, including defensive backs Ronnie Lott, Carlton Williamson, and Eric Wright, all picked by Walsh in the1981 draft.

"Bill has a nice touch in the draft," said 49ers vice president Ken Flower in 1985. "I don't know exactly what it is, but it's like what they say about a great passer: he has a great touch.

Former Oakland Raiders executive Al LoCasale said more.

"You win with people in this league, and Walsh has the people. He's a creative coach, sure, but the key to the 49ers is the players that Walsh has brought in."

Flower noted that Walsh was surrounded by skilled football people, but made all the final decisions in the draft.

"Bill is always looking for players who excel in something, some little part of the game or some character trait, even though they aren't well-regarded overall."

Walsh also had a keen eye for free agents. The two best were Hicks, who had been cut by two teams, and aging linebacker Jack "Hacksaw" Reynolds, who had been released by the Los Angeles Rams after 11 seasons. Reynolds was short (5-foot-11) and thickset (232 pounds), the prototype of the middle linebacker in the run-to-daylight era of the '70s. The Rams wanted quicker, bigger linebackers in their new 3-4 alignment. Reynolds had lost a step at 33 but could still read plays and shed blockers. Indeed, he'd read and shed in Super Bowl XVI, making one of the biggest tackles of his career on Cincinnati fullback Pete Johnson a yard from the end zone.

Besides his smarts and fire, Reynolds was a unique competitor. Before home games, he would drive to Candlestick Park in full uniform, arriving hours ahead of his teammates. On the road, Reynolds would attend the pregame meal wearing his uniform and a mean look.

"He was the most intense player you'll ever see," said Walsh. "He was consumed with football. Now, if there is anybody who inspired you, there it is. You're sitting there eating and he's in full uniform, ready to go.

Reynolds got his nickname at the University of Tennessee after losing a game to Archie Manning and Ole Miss, 36–0. Still fuming a few days later, Reynolds found a 1953 Chevrolet and whipped out a hacksaw. It took two days and a dozen blades, but Reynolds kept hacking away and finally cut the frame in half.

"I really work for myself," he once said, "If everyone does that, busting his ass, well, collectively you'll really have something."

Among Walsh's other pickups were tight end Russ Francis, linebacker Matt Millen, pass rushers Fred Dean and Charles Haley, kicker Ray Wersching, and halfbacks Lenvil Elliott and Bill Ring.

In Seifert's eight seasons with the 49ers, they won two Super Bowls (XXIV and XXIX) and 75 percent of their games (108–35), including playoff contests. But there were also five seasons that ended with playoff losses, four of them to advancing teams in Dallas and Green Bay. There was also the awkward and sometimes heated quarterback controversy involving Montana and Young.

When Montana was struggling with back and elbow injuries, Young gave the 49ers an extra gear with his powerful runs and his deep passes.

George Seifert, who succeeded Walsh as head coach, and Steve Young, who replaced Montana at quarterback.

Young was also a formidable competitor. In a game against Pittsburgh, which the 49erss won, he allowed linebacker Kevin Greene to knock him to the ground just after the whistle had sounded.

"I thought I could get a 15-yard penalty," he later explained.

There were any number of reasons the 49ers started to slip after Seifert's second Super Bowl win, a 49–26 rout of the San Diego Chargers in which Steve Young threw six touchdown passes. The two biggest obstacles to the championship had been Dallas and Green Bay. Each of those teams had added quarterbacks who would become Hall of Famers: Brett Favre with the Packers and Troy Aikman with the Cowboys. The 49ers' future had been placed with quarterback Jim Druckenmiller, a first-round bust in 1997. The same year they passed on Jake Plummer. Three years later, the 49ers overlooked future Hall of Fame quarterback Tom Brady (as did 29 other teams).

There were also some poor overall drafts during the years when the 49ers were an aging team. Two other division teams, St. Louis and Seattle, which came over from the AFC West in the 2002 realignment, improved dramatically with the addition of new coaches; the Seahawks' new mentor was Mike Holmgren, the former 49ers offensive coordinator. Yet, the biggest factor in the 49ers' decline was the arrival of free agency and a salary cap, both designed to theoretically make each of the 32 teams end up with 8–8 records. During the 49ers' run to five Super Bowls, owner Eddie DeBartolo was extremely generous with pay increases and bonuses and, until 1994, he'd never had to cope with a salary cap.

"He was very generous," said former assistant coach Bill McPherson. "I felt like I was part of the family when I was over there. Sometimes he would get on us. Even if we won and the score wasn't bigger than he expected, he'd get on us. He was so *attached* to the team. He might be crying before a game. He treated us like we were part of a family. If you had a money problem or someone was sick, he'd take care of it. Eddie was the guy. He kept the team going."

Most teams were slow to realize how much the salary cap and free agency were going to dramatically change the structure of the league.

"It kind of looked like a backlash to what happened in '94, where people who had a vested interest were beginning to see where players were willing to sign with teams for reasons other than money," said Policy, the 49ers' president. "Now, it [free agency] throws the system out of kilter."

Policy insisted that the 49ers were "in the middle of the pack" regarding spending. Of course, the cap doesn't include money spent on hotel, air fare, and other expenditures that Eddie DeBartolo lavished on his athletes.

"The experience we went through in the '80s, you'll notice there was a time when Bill [Walsh] was able to wheel and deal rather regularly in some of the early drafts," said Policy. "But then teams stopped dealing with the 49ers, even if the compensation was even greater than what they they'd get from another team, because they didn't want to deal with the Niners."

DeBartolo had made a habit of handing out playoff bonuses and doubling the salaries of key players. There were also "loans" during the 1987 player's strike that were never repaid. At one point, the league stepped in and fined DeBartolo $50,000. While all of this shadowy, but legal dealing was going on, the Minnesota Vikings jumped into the debate and slammed the 49ers for their free-spending; in the mid-'80s, the 49ers had the league's largest payroll at $14.5 million, while the Vikings had the lowest at $8.5 million.

"San Francisco is doing more harm than the USFL in escalating salaries," said Vikings general manager Mike Lynn, referring to the ill-fated rival United States Football League. "I don't know how they can issue a contract like that to unproven players, then look at some seven-year players in the eye." Lynn was talking about linebacker Jim Fahnhorst, a Vikings draftee who signed with the USFL but returned to the NFL with the 49ers when he was offered a four-year, $1.545 million deal. "Tell him to mind his own business and try to build a winner up there," cracked DeBartolo, "We've won a couple of Super Bowls. They've been a bridesmaid all their life."

While all of this sniping was going on, George Seifert was trying to produce a fifth Super Bowl after DeBartolo had issued his ultimatum: a Super Bowl without Joe Montana, who had been traded to the Kansas City Chiefs on April 20, 1993. The Montana trade staggered 49ers fans. There had been the serious back and elbow injuries he had suffered, forcing him to surrender the West Coast offense to Steve Young. But Montana, a fast healer, had always made amazing recoveries from surgery, revealing his gritty determination to continue playing a very dangerous game. The plan all along had been to replace Montana with Young, with Montana remaining as a skilled backup. But Montana was unwilling to surrender his job, and that prompted the blockbuster trade.

Two years after Montana left, Young led the 49ers to their fifth Super Bowl win, a 49–26 blowout of the San Diego Chargers. It was Steve Young's Oscar game. Young threw a Super Bowl record six touchdown passes, continually burning the San Diego safeties. Jerry Rice took one of his passes for a 4-yard score just 1:24 into the game. At the time, it was the fastest touchdown in Super Bowl history.

In the past, the 49ers would have rewarded their champions with bonuses and pay raises, while the promise of more Super Bowl rings hung in the air amidst the confetti and bright lights. But it was now a different time, a different system, and three key players—corners Deion Sanders and Eric Davis and running back Ricky Watters—had jumped to other teams for more money. With moves like that, it was fast becoming obvious that winning a Super Bowl was much, much tougher than it had been before the NFL players union gained a free agency system and the owners won a salary cap clause that restricted the amount a team could spend on talent. (Carmen Policy was one of the first executives to see a way of beating the cap by prorating signing bonuses as part of a player's package.)

When the 49ers lost back-to-back playoffs to Green Bay following the 1995 and 1996 seasons, DeBartolo fired Seifert. Seifert's overall record by then was 108–35. He had given the 49ers eight straight seasons of double-digit wins and a winning percentage of 75.5. Yet it wasn't enough. Policy left, too, joining the Cleveland Browns expansion franchise in 1998.

The upheaval in the 49ers' front office showed how difficult it had become to win a Super Bowl under the free agency/cap system. And it showed the heartaches and consequences of not repeating after your team has gotten its first one. Perhaps realizing that, George Seifert hung out his "Gone fishin'" sign and climbed aboard his 23-foot Grady White, a gift from owner Eddie DeBartolo after Super Bowl XXIV. The boat was named *Flip 3* after the defensive formula used by the 49ers' secondary in the early '80s.

Of course, Seifert would always come out a runner-up to Bill Walsh in any popularity contest. But Seifert had something extra: his memories of growing up in San Francisco and watching the 49ers play at aging Kezar Stadium. He used to work games as an usher, sometimes collecting the chinstraps of R. C. Owens, Matt Hazeltine, and Billy Wilson.

"I remember when the 49ers lost to Detroit in a playoff game, 31–27 after leading 27–7," he recalled. "I was in high school, my senior year. To see that thing unfold and remember the hush over the city following the game . . . . There was a quiet that was indescribable."

Seifert was happily in retirement with his family, his memories, and his fishing gear when the Carolina Panthers came calling in 1999. The Panthers were a fifth-year expansion team with former NFL star Jerry Richardson as their ambitious owner. Richardson liked Seifert's resume and record for shutting down offenses when the 49ers offense stumbled. Seifert liked the owner's football background and became excited about coaching and building a new team. They shook hands, and Seifert was back in the game he'd loved since those childhood days at Kezar.

One of Seifert's first acts as the new Panthers coach was to hang a quote from Teddy Roosevelt on the wall behind his desk:

It is not the critic who counts; not the man who points out how the strong man stumbles or where the doer of deeds could have done better. The credit belongs to the man who is actually in the arena, whose face is marred with dust and sweat and blood, who strives valiantly, who errs and comes up short again and again because there is no effort without error or shortcoming.

With veteran quarterback Steve Beuerlein running his offense, Seifert's first two seasons were marked by promise with records of 8–8 and 7–9. The Panthers defeated the 49ers twice in each season, with an outbreak of 144 points behind Beuerlein. But then the future, once so promising, collapsed, when Seifert released Beuerlein and turned the quarterback job over to Jeff Lewis. Lewis was later cut before the season, leaving rookie Chris Weinke, a fourth-round draft pick, as the new starter. The result was a dreadful 1–15 season, one win at the top, then 15 straight losses. Seifert was fired the day after the final game, a 38–6 loss to New England. Seifert, a victim perhaps of free agency, appeared to vanish after that dismal season.

After the Panthers' twelfth straight loss, a 25–24 squeaker at Buffalo, Seifert came up with this memorable quote: "The problem here is that we haven't solved the problem. And it's been an ongoing problem." Seifert issued another funny one-liner to future Pro Bowl defensive end Julius Peppers. Seifert quipped, "Out of something bad [his 1–15 record] came something good [a high first-round draft pick], right?"

And, so, George Seifert was through with the wildly unpredictable game of pro football. Except for one 49ers home game each year, he resumed devoting himself to his family and the outdoors.

"I'm fishing, hunting, enjoying the outdoors, and playing with my grandchildren, all the stuff you are supposed to do in retirement," he said.

CHAPTER 10

JOE LEAVES A SADDENED CITY

AFTER THEIR SUPER Bowl blitz under Bill Walsh, the 49ers started to age. Quarterback Joe Montana, their inspirational leader, began struggling with injuries, undergoing back and elbow surgery and suffering at least two concussions.

After Montana endured back surgery in 1986, he made an amazing recovery, missing only seven games. Yet Walsh knew he needed a better backup than Jeff Kemp and went shopping. His trail led to Tampa, where he found Steve Young, a skilled but unhappy prospect.

Young was a bigger, stronger quarterback than Montana with better running skills, but he'd played only one season as a starter on a 2–14 team. He had been sacked 68 times in two seasons and was only a 53-percent passer. Yet Walsh sensed that Young was a very talented quarterback playing on a disorganized, demoralized team. So Carmen Policy, carrying a load of Eddie DeBartolo's money, made a million-dollar cash deal that proved to be the bargain of the century, "a steal," as the 49ers' opponents put it.

As Montana began missing games, Young stepped in and kept the 49ers at the top of their division.

"Joe had been in there for so long that the team didn't know where to go," said Young. "The players had a loyalty to Joe, but, after a while, they had to respond to a different style. The team began wondering, *Do we look at Steve as a replacement, or do we look at Steve as the quarterback?*"

In 1992, Montana underwent a second surgery on his elbow after the first game. He didn't play the rest of the season, as Young put up some impressive numbers: 25 touchdowns, only seven interceptions, a quarterback rating of 107.0, and his first Pro Bowl appearance. Accordingly, it didn't take long for Montana's name to come up when beat writers were digging for offseason stories and management was a little more willing to certify the rumors. Carmen Policy confirmed that several teams had inquired about Montana. One of them was Kansas City, an AFC team that had been circling the Super Bowl sites, looking for a parking place.

The Chiefs, who had gone 23 years without a Super Bowl appearance, were competing in a conference stocked with star quarterbacks: John Elway in Denver, Jim Kelly in Buffalo, Dan Marino in Miami, and Warren Moon in Houston. Policy told the Chiefs he was seeking a first-round draft choice in return for the 36-year-old Montana. Eventually he got it, a pick the 49ers used to draft defensive tackle Dana Stubblefield, a future Pro Bowler.

The reaction of 49ers fans to the loss of Joe Montana was fast and furious, sad and nostalgic. They remembered the down seasons, and how Montana had brought the city out of its despair in those exciting Super Bowl years. They remembered how Montana had played through pain and bruises, and how he had brought the 49ers back in so many big games, including the drama-packed Super Bowl XXIII with that last-minute touchdown pass to John Taylor.

The fans had lived and suffered each time Montana would need surgery. In 1996, after Montana suffered a ruptured disc in his back, Vince Bell of San Francisco probably said it best for every 49ers fan: "Aw, this is *horrible*," said Bell. "The body can take only so much. I feel like sending him flowers."

A *USA Today* headline summed it all up: "Montana's Calamity Shakes San Francisco."

To say that Joe Montana was a treasure in San Francisco would not be an overstatement. Some of the fans openly wept when hearing about the trade. Others were angry. All of them were stunned by the decision to let a legendary quarterback leave their city instead of letting him retire as a 49er with a very special ceremony.

The tributes would follow, but it would come only after Montana had finished his remarkable career with a two-year farewell in Kansas City.

Eddie DeBartolo, of course, had wanted Montana to stay. Carmen Policy had cited the Chiefs' offering of a first-round draft pick and Montana approaching the age of 37. Finally, as the trade talks dominated the call-in shows and street talk, DeBartolo and Policy agreed to let Montana decide his own fate. In effect, they were conceding that Young was now the 49ers' starting quarterback, but Montana was in no mood to sit on the bench and hold a clipboard for Young.

"If I go to Kansas City, I'll be the man," he said. "If I get injured, they'll pray for me to get well. If I get hurt here, I'll be pushed out the door."

The trade was finalized on April 20, 1993. In his second season, Montana would lead the Chiefs to an emotional 24–17 win over the 49ers. Later that season, the 49ers would win their fifth Super Bowl, a 49–26 blowout of San Diego, as Young threw a record six touchdown passes.

When he first arrived in Kansas City, Montana received front-page headlines and was the lead story on all the television stations. He drew crowds and young autograph seekers everywhere he went. His next-door family even threw a welcome party in his honor. If any well-wishers lingered outside of Montana's new home, its location revealed by a local gossip columnist, those same neighbors would make sure they didn't linger for long.

"You get concerned about what people are going to do, said Montana. "But our neighbors have been great. They are really watching out for us. It's given us a very comfortable feeling, like we are wanted."

Even before Montana had thrown his first pass for the Chiefs, he was treated like a movie star. There were four varieties of Montana

Joe Montana wanted to keep playing even after his injuries and was traded to Kansas City.

T-shirts available at local stores. His No. 19 jersey quickly became a best-seller. (Montana wore that number because his former No. 16 jersey, once worn by Hall of Fame quarterback Len Dawson, had been retired. Montana's new number, it turned out, had once been worn by Titus Dixon, a 152-pound free agent wide receiver.)

"I've never seen anything like it in this in town," said Kansas City sportscaster Bob Gretz. "These people can't get enough of Joe Montana. I wonder what will happen if the Chiefs really are successful."

There was no argument about what was on the minds of those Kansas City fans. They had suffered through more than twenty years since the Chiefs had won Super Bowl IV in an upset over the Minnesota Vikings. And now they had Montana, a veteran of the Super Bowl wars, who had won four of them and never thrown a single interception.

Confronted by these lofty expectations, Chiefs Coach Marty Schottenheimer was quick to divorce himself and his team from the subject.

"You know, that's something that's never been discussed around here," he said. "That's just something that . . . because he's been a guy who has four Super Bowl rings, three MVP trophies, and he's coming to a pretty good football team, that's kind of been around the edges, but not here. So that's a very natural expectation. But the principal reasons that we obtained Joe Montana were (a) we thought he was still a pretty good football player, and (b), we thought his presence might well accelerate the transition to our new offense."

Then Schottenheimer began talking about the skills of his new quarterback.

"His vision and his anticipation are just amazing," the coach said. "You know, when he first came here and we watched him practice for the first time, somebody noticed that the ball would come out of his hand and be headed towards the middle of the field on a crossing route and there wouldn't be anybody there. And then, all of a sudden, here'd come this guy, and the ball would be right on target. He's still a terrific athlete. I mean, for 37 years old, he's got very good athletic ability in terms of movement and body control."

And how did Montana feel after his early workouts with the Chiefs?

"It's been kind of intense, but it's been fun," he said, "It's been a nice change for me . . . just being able to play again."

In any discussion about the future of the Chiefs with Montana as their new catalyst were these startling facts: The Chiefs had finished twenty-fifth in offense and gave up 48 sacks the previous year.

"It's been overwhelming," said general manager Carl Peterson. "Expectations have gotten way out of control."

Yet Montana himself didn't try to quiet all the talk of a Super Bowl.

"Can't say I disagree with the talk," he said. "I'm playing to get to another Super Bowl. That's why I'm back. Why shouldn't this team do it?"

In Montana's two seasons, the Chiefs would qualify for the playoffs with records of 11–5 and 9–7. But a struggling Montana, reaching back for his old big-game skills, found that Jerry Rice and John Taylor were missing, that Bill Walsh was far away in another time zone, and that his own skills weren't what they used to be.

The Chiefs were ousted by Buffalo, 30–13, in the 1993 AFC title game, and by Miami 27–17 in the first round in 1994, and then it was all over for Joe Montana. Meanwhile, the 49ers were celebrating their fifth Super Bowl championship as Steve Young picked apart San Diego's confused pass defense, just the way Montana had in his prime years. (From 1991 to '94, Young threw 109 touchdown passes and was intercepted only 41 times.)

Yet, in the minds of most 49ers fans, Montana was still the hero they worshipped. As Bill Walsh once said, "Joe is like a stiletto—quick, daring, refined, almost technically and mechanically perfect, and the entire 49er offense is based on that style, systematically taking apart a defense. He has to make far more decisions than, say, John Elway, but he's more equipped to do it." Former commentator John Madden agreed. "He never struggled with it," said Madden. "He never fought it. He just did it so fluidly and easily, and the higher the stakes, the calmer he played."

The fans weren't the only ones who felt a strong attachment to Montana and the Chiefs after he left. Most of the 49ers huddled around a television screen to watch Montana spark a comeback win over the Houston Oilers.

"We were excited," said 49er guard Guy McIntyre. "I think it was because a lot of us played with him and wanted to see him have continued success. Joe was such a big part of this organization for so long and orchestrated so many winning drives for us. So it's just natural. Nobody wanted him to go out and fail."

Not everybody was so attached. Fullback Tom Rathman took a tougher approach to what he was seeing on the screen.

"What's Joe got to do with our Dallas game?" said Rathman. "Focus, baby. First things first."

In retirement, Montana reflected on his feelings and how he came to be known as "Joe Cool." "Before big games, it wasn't anything in my stomach, just nervous excitement, not wanting to let anyone down," he said. "I couldn't wait for the first hit. Until you get hit, you still have the nervous adrenaline going. I was like, *Please, I don't care if someone hits me late and knocks me down, just get the first hit over with.*"

Montana's favorite Super Bowl had been Bill Walsh's last, that dramatic 20–16 victory over the Cincinnati Bengals.

"When you're a kid playing in your backyard, you always win the Super Bowl on the last play," he said. "And to have that come true, it was fun."

As skilled and competitive as Joe Montana was, there was one aspect of his career in which he always trailed Steve Young: money. In 1982, the NFL Players Association bargained the right to review every player contract. Union figures revealed that Montana earned $325,000. It was his fourth season. He had already won a Super Bowl. Yet Montana was earning less than Archie Manning ($600,000) or Craig Morton ($330,000), neither of whom had ever won a Super Bowl.

Meanwhile, in 1984, Young decided to jump to the Los Angeles Express of the fledgling United States Football League, an easy jump as it turned out. Express owner J. William Oldenburg was so passionate about fielding a team of college stars that he gave Young, a Mormon, a staggering $40 million contract that stretched over 43 years. Moreover, Oldenburg guaranteed every dollar of the most lucrative contract in professional sports history. (Ironically, it turned out, Oldenburg's IMI Corporation was located in San Francisco.)

According to various reports, Young's contract included a yearly salary of $1.3 million for five years, a $1 million signing bonus, a $1 million interest-free loan, a $100,000 a year endorsement loan, a 20-year $200,000 scholarship fund for Young's college, Brigham Young University, and an undetermined fee for each Express victory to be donated to community youth groups in the Los Angeles area.

"I wanted to able to give back some of the things that were given to me at BYU the last four years," said Young. "And I can do that now through the tough decision, obviously, and it took much deliberation on my part. I've always wanted to play in the NFL, but at times it seemed like they really didn't want me that badly. In the end, the Express showed that they were devoted to me, and I followed my heart."

The Express team, citing poor attendance, folded after Young's second season. The USFL also disbanded after its television-driven monopoly lawsuit against the NFL was rejected in 1986. Young was selected by Tampa Bay in a special dispersal draft, then was traded a year later, giving the 49ers a Montana-Young quarterback combo, perhaps the best in NFL history.

Here's how one NFL scouting report evaluated Young:

Super competitor. Exceptional athlete, runner, and scrambler. Can buy time with his feet and run for positive yardage. Tough, elusive, and nifty. Has taken some good hits and doesn't shy away from contact. Has great feel for when to stay in the pocket and when to scramble. Throws the ball as accurately as any college quarterback I have ever seen. Has rare anticipation and toughness. Makes excellent reads. Can unload quickly. Gets the most out of himself. Negatives: A little shorter than you'd like (6-01/2). Lacks a cannon arm. Some of his deep passes will hang. Throws too many high passes over the middle. Notes: Left-handed passer. Great-great-great-grandson of Mormon colonizer Brigham Young. Set NCAA records in 1983 for total offense and completion percentage.

It took Young eight years to win his own Super Bowl while putting up some impressive individual numbers quarterbacking Bill Walsh's West Coast offense. In the two seasons after Montana left, Young passed for 3,465 and 4,023 yards, once throwing 183 passes in a row without an interception. Yet, 49ers loyalists would never be satisfied with mere passing stats, gaudy as they were. They wanted another Super Bowl championship. Young gave it to them in 1994, with a spectacular postseason.

***

Why is the NFL's Super Bowl regarded as the most emotional of all major championships and perhaps the toughest to win? The answer is simple. Unlike baseball, basketball, and hockey, which conduct seven-game series to crown their champions, the Super Bowl winner is decided on one emotionally charged evening in which one bad play can determine which team receives those gleaming championship rings and the coveted Vince Lombardi trophy.

Tex Schramm, who used to run the Dallas Cowboys, has had more than his share of heartbreaking plays in lost Super Bowls.

"We never remember the great wins," Schramm once said. "All we remember are the bad plays, the bad games."

Former Miami Coach Don Shula once said that the Super Bowl loser gets "thrown back on the pile with all the other teams that didn't get there."

Each year, the Super Bowl numerals are reminders of bad Sundays. There are vivid memories of the Benny Barnes tripping call that doomed the Cowboys in Super Bowl XIII. The Duane Thomas goal-line fumble that cost the Cowboys another win in Super Bowl V. The Earl Morrall flea-flicker mistake in Super Bowl III. The Lewis Billups juggle that deprived Cincinnati of an upset win in Super Bowl XXIII.

Sam Wyche was a winning coach with three minutes to play in Super Bowl XXIII. But Joe Montana drove the 49ers 92 yards for the winning touchdown, and Wyche was a heartbroken loser. There had been three haunting moments when Wyche thought he would win.

"Once Joe [Montana] came back to his second receiver, John Taylor, I think," Wyche recalled. "Lewis [Billups] was right there with his fingers spread looking right at the ball. It was like a person trying to catch a balloon. It wouldn't stick. If he catches it, we kneel down and the game is ours.

"Earlier on the drive, Montana threw for Jerry Rice on second-and-20 yards. We triple-teamed Jerry Rice," said Wyche. "David Fulcher had him long. Lewis Billups had him short. Ray Horton was in what we call a lurking position. Ray slipped, and somehow Joe got the ball inside to Rice, who picked up 32 yards."

And there was Montana's game-winner, a dramatic 10-yarder to Taylor with 34 seconds left to play.

"If you look at the end-zone shot, [it] said inches, the farthest maybe 10 inches. Montana threw an absolutely perfect pass. It was one of those times you played the what-if game 1,000 times a year, where you're just a step away."

Schramm's Cowboys lost three Super Bowl squeakers on mistakes, one of them that Benny Barnes tripping call, perhaps the worst in Super Bowl history and one that enabled Pittsburgh to win, 35–31. That same Bowl game, Jackie Smith, a 38-year-old tight end brought out of retirement, dropped what should have been a touchdown pass. And there was the Duane Thomas fumble in Super Bowl V, an agonizing 16–13 loss to the Baltimore Colts.

"Yeah, I've had a lot of sick moments," Schramm once said. "If we win those two Super Bowls, we're the team of the century."

Lindy Infante, Cincinnati's former offensive coordinator, knows the same sinking feeling. With the 49ers leading in Super Bowl XVI, the Bengals had a first down at the San Francisco 3 yard line. What followed were almost all muscle plays. Three runs by jumbo back Pete Johnson. A little third-down swing pass to Charles Alexander. The Bengals, who lost the game 26–21, left the ball and their Super Bowl dreams at the 1 yard line.

Infante always refused to second-guess himself.

"As a play caller, you call over 1,000 plays a year," he said. "You've got five, six, seven seconds to do it. If any play caller lets himself be second-guessed on the basis of one play, he's in big trouble. A 250-pound back couldn't get a yard? Whose fault is that? I've always said that no one play, or no one player, ever wins or loses a football game. It's a three, three-and-a-half hour, multi-faceted game."

Yet, the history of numerous lost Super Bowls seems to be filled with memories of single plays.

The Bengals' stall against the 49ers came in 1982, the same year Dionne Warwick recorded her hit record "Heartbreaker," the anthem of the losers of close Super Bowls.

***

In the 14 seasons that Joe Montana directed the 49ers offense, he suffered more than his share of injuries to his elbow, knees, spine, wrist, and ribs. Quarterbacks take more hits than any other player for the obvious reason: They handle the ball on every play except for punts and kicks. But think about this: The quarterback is also the only offensive player who begins a play moving *backwards*, whether from a shotgun formation or from under center.

Montana's injuries produced some frightening headlines: "Montana Is Hospitalized for Concussion;" "Montana Undergoes Major Back Surgery;" "Back Injury Puts Montana's Career in Peril;" "Montana in Stable Condition." Yet, Montana himself always shrugged off the pain and the endless hours in the trainer's room as just part of the game.

"I guess people forget that injuries are part of the game," he said. "They tend to play them up a little more. I don't really understand that because, you know, it isn't a non-contact sport. It's pretty physical. So guys are going to get hurt."

"Joe Montana is one of the truly courageous performers of our time," said Bill Walsh. "He has nerve. He has instinct. He has a certain command. He's got a lot of confidence in doing those things that he's been doing probably since high school. He thoroughly thrives on football. He's the essence of the game itself."

Montana's injuries became so frequent that some newspapers began listing them by years:

- 1984—Missed his first start in 49 games against Philadelphia because of a bruised sternum.
- 1985—Missed a wild-card playoff game against the New York Giants with a shoulder injury.
- 1986—Injured his back in the season opener against Tampa Bay and missed eight games with a ruptured disc. Extensive examinations revealed a condition known as "congenital spinal stenosis associated with an acute rupture of the L5-S1 disc." He was operated on to widen the canal and remove the ruptured disc. Montana returned after missing eight games.
- 1987—Missed a game with Atlanta because of a pulled hamstring. Missed part of a game against New Orleans because of a hand injury.
- 1988—Bruised his elbow in the opener against New Orleans. Suffered injured ribs against Denver. Missed a game with Minnesota because of a back injury.
- 1989—Injured his right elbow against New Orleans and missed the following game against Dallas. Injured his left knee against New England. Missed the next game with the New York Jets because of a knee injury.
- 1990—Missed a game with New Orleans because of a strained lower abdominal. Received a broken finger and bruised sternum against the New York Giants in the NFC title game.
- 1991—Missed the entire season with tendonitis of his right elbow. Injured his sternum and suffered a broken finger against the Los Angeles Rams in the NFC title game.

Montana himself dismisses his injuries as just part of a very physical game.

"I don't think I've taken any more beating than anybody else," he said before Super Bowl XXIII. "I like the game and I like playing it."

In 1986, he suffered a back injury in the opener against Tampa Bay that was so severe that it required disc surgery. There were all of those scary career-ending stories, including this observation from Michael Dillingham, the team physician, who said, "There is a chance that he won't play football again. I think there is a consensus that Joe *will* play again, but there is also the risk that, even if the surgery is successful, it won't relieve that pain."

Yet, 56 days after the surgery, guess who was trotting out to take the 49ers' first offensive snap against the St. Louis Cardinals—and not only take snaps, but throw three touchdown passes to Jerry Rice and pass for 270 yards in a 43–17 win.

"Not to knock [backups] Mike Moroski or Jeff Kemp," said veteran guard Randy Cross, "but we've gone an awful lot of places with Joe Montana. It was just the fact that we had him back again. It seemed like old times out there."

Montana himself was thrilled, but muted his excitement.

"I was just glad to be back," he said, after absorbing eight hits without feeling any pain. "If you are afraid of getting hit or hurt, then you are going to get hurt. Once the game started, it was too late to start worrying about it."

So dominant was Montana's offense that the 49ers didn't have to punt until the fourth quarter. On the first seven possessions, Montana led the offense to three touchdowns and three field goals.

"It felt good to throw the football deep," he said. "There was a place deep down within me where I thought I couldn't reach. But I didn't feel anything on the long one to Jerry [a 45-yard touchdown pass to Rice], and it gave me a lot of confidence."

Wide receiver Dwight Clark said Montana had been nervous about his future before his back surgery. "But he was confident," said Clark. "He said the doctors told him that it [the disc] was pressing against his nerve and something had to be done. I was devastated. I thought at first he had to be kidding."

Walsh reacted to Montana's surgery by suggesting that his light-weight quarterback add 10 pounds in the offseason.

"More than anything, Joe's loss of weight through surgery affected him the most," said Walsh, referring to the way Montana ran stiffly and lacked the same zip on his passes. "He never really gained it back. And he wasn't as strong as he was accustomed to."

Sam Wyche, Montana's quarterback coach in his early years, said he wasn't surprised at Montana's ability and nerve in coming back from injuries.

"It's the nature of almost every position," he said, "That's what the league is dealing with now. Most injuries occur when you get two opposing players playing at different speeds. You even see linemen, coming out of a block and slowing down and another lineman running up his back—one is going full-speed, the other is slowing down. Joe is such a competitor. He's so determined that he's not going to be out one day longer than he needs to. Some people don't like to be laying around."

In 1986, the season in which Montana underwent his back surgery, 10 other starting quarterbacks were sidelined by various injuries. The Chicago Bears used quarterbacks Jim McMahon, Mike Tomczak, Steve Fuller, and Doug Flutie during an injury-filled season. Yet, the defending Super Bowl champions used a relentless defense to finish with a 10–5–1 regular season record and reach the divisional playoffs.

After that outbreak of injuries, and after only eight quarterbacks started all 16 games, the NFL Competition Committee voted to strengthen the rules on roughing the passer.

"It's a tough game," said Shula, the Miami Dolphins' head coach. "We're not trying to put skirts on the quarterback. We just want to tighten it up."

CHAPTER 11

EDDIE LOSES HIS TEAM

EDDIE DEBARTOLO SHOULD have known better. He'd grown up as the son of a billionaire mall developer who'd taught him the basics of the business world. He was a graduate of Notre Dame. He'd been smart enough to hire Bill Walsh when he owned the San Francisco 49ers. But he made a terrible mistake and played a down-and-dirty game when seeking a casino riverboat license.

There was a clandestine meeting with former Louisiana governor Edwin Edwards at a Baton Rouge hotel bar. There was a $400,000 cash payoff outside a San Francisco hotel. And there was an elated feeling the next day when DeBartolo was awarded the license that Edwards had swung his way. The riverboat was to be the anchor for a $250 million retail project in Bossier City, Louisiana.

"It was a mistake, a mistake that very well could have ruined my life," DeBartolo later said. "It had a terrible impact on my life and my family, and it was a mistake. And I'll say it again. The biggest mistake I made was not paying by check. But he didn't want a check, he wanted cash."

DeBartolo eventually pleaded guilty in October 1998 for failing to report a felony, then agreed to testify against Edwards.

"It was plain and simple extortion," he said. "I was a victim of his threats."

Under federal law, DeBartolo's mistake is known as "misprision of a felony." DeBartolo's lawyer, Aubrey Harwell, insisted there was a "fundamental sense of unfairness of him pleading to anything." DeBartolo, however, says the sentence—two years of probation and a $1 million fine—was fair. The probation terms included several visits each year to probation officers in Tampa, his new home, and San Francisco.

"I have unlimited travel so I don't have to tell anybody when I leave, or if I leave, Tampa," DeBartolo said.

But then came the jarring aftermath. Because of his felony, DeBartolo was ousted from his ownership of the 49ers. Since he rarely attended league meetings, DeBartolo had few friends among the NFL owners he could call for support. Thus, Denise DeBartolo York, his sister, gained control of the team and immediately began a major cost-cutting project.

This was no first-rounder in the brother-sister family feud. DeBartolo York, a petite, attractive, shy woman, was married to retired entrepreneur John York.

"John gave me the strength, the guts, to finally do what was right," she told the *San Francisco Chronicle*. "To not cave in and die and lose everything. I had to clear our good name."

In 1999, on the advice of tax attorneys, DeBartolo York filed a $150 million suit to recover $94 million in debt that Eddie owed the corporation. Her brother countered by filing a $150 million suit against his sister, seeking damages. "I placed my trust and my family's financial future in Denise's hands, and that trust has been betrayed," said Eddie.

An incident involving several photos of Eddie with Bill Walsh celebrating Super Bowl victories only worsened the brother-sister relationship, when the pictures had suddenly vanished from the trophy case at the 49ers' headquarters.

"The guy I had sent out, one of the controllers, had taken my brother's pictures down," she told the *Chronicle*. "I couldn't believe he did that. And I got blamed for it. That is so far from the truth."

The controller referenced was DeBartolo Corporation CPA and 49ers vice president Keith Lenhart.

"Eddie isn't involved with the team anymore," said Lenhart, when asked to explain his action.

Denise learned of the incident in a phone call, when she and her husband were flying to New Orleans for a 49ers game. She reportedly became ill when she discovered that the story was being reported in the San Francisco newspapers.

"People who know me know I would never do that," she said. "It was horrible, just unbelievable. I mean, my brother is part of that team's history. Because you take a picture out, it doesn't go away. I don't operate like that. If I could have anything come out of all of this, it would be for my life to get back to normal, as much as it can, and for all of us to be a family again."

Meanwhile, far from the hills of San Francisco, Eddie DeBartolo has restructured his life without those thrilling weekends when Joe Montana was leading the 49ers to another win and closer to another Super Bowl. He sold his home on the San Francisco Peninsula and moved to a new mansion in Tampa. Edward DeBartolo Sr., who had built a development and management empire before his death in 1994, had constructed 15 malls in the Tampa-Orlando area, and, in 1976, he came close to buying the Tampa Bay expansion franchise, so Eddie knew the area.

"I feel good, I love Florida," said Eddie Jr.. He shops for groceries, enjoys takeout Chinese dinners with his wife, Candy, and daughters Lisa and Nikki. But deep in the mind of Eddie DeBartolo, deep where the memories of Joe Montana and windblown Sundays at Candlestick Park are lodged, he misses the thrill and glare of pro football.

"Isn't life strange?" he said, referring to his trial. "I felt bad for everything he [Edwards] did and for all the problems that he caused me with the NFL . . . with my family, with a lot of things. But justice was served. Sometimes it's served cold, sometimes warm. But it was served."

DeBartolo insists that he could still be involved as an owner, but decided to turn the 49ers over to his sister.

"Commissioner [Paul] Tagliabue did, obviously, suspend me," he said. "But as I was going through negotiations with my family, and we went through negotiations with the lawyers, it did not come down to the team being *taken*. It came down to a decision that had to be made whether or not I wanted the 49ers or whether or not I wanted the other part of the condition. And I decided that it would be best if I took the other side and my tenure with the 49ers would end then at that time.

"I had success and done a lot with the 49ers. It meant the world to me. But I figured with my daughters and with them getting older and having grandchildren at the time and them planning on families, what would be best for me to do was to be a good grandfather, be a good husband and do what I want to do, maybe travel a little bit, spend more time with my family."

Denise DeBartolo York continues to try to bring some sense of purpose to this ongoing feud.

"You know what I resent the most from all of this?" she offered. "I resent any of this happening. It fell into my lap: the 49ers, the accusations, and the scrutiny—all of it. Eddie blew my cover. He blew my cover."

She now oversees the huge business empire started by her father Edward DeBartolo Sr..

"I've never said much. I stayed in the background until Eddie got into the predicament," she said.

In her reorganization of the 49ers, Denise listed herself and husband, John, as cochairmen. Jeb, her son, was named the team's CEO. The organization also included 19 directors, including one for the museum and for the theatre at the team's Levi's Stadium. Eddie's club officials had listed Eddie as board chairman and only three directors. In fact, Eddie's entire office staff numbered only twelve members, including Bill Walsh as president and head coach. Denise was not mentioned.

Since 2000, when DeBartolo York and her husband took over control of the team and began their massive cost-cutting operation, the 49ers have endured 11 losing seasons and seven head coaches, and left their fans wondering when the embarrassment will end. They remember the thrilling Sundays at Candlestick Park. They remember Joe Montana throwing those perfect spirals and pulling off games that he had no right to pull off.

Candlestick Park is gone, too. One year after a symbolic final pass was thrown—Montana to Eddie DeBartolo at the end of a "Legends of Candlestick" celebrity flag football game in the summer of 2014—the stadium was demolished. It was only a short throw that DeBartolo caught, but that was fitting since the foundation of the West Coast offense was the short, snappy pass. The players then carried DeBartolo off the field on their shoulders. Cincinnati's Hall of Fame offensive

Candlestick Park was demolished after a ceremonial flag football game in 2014.

tackle Anthony Munoz, who lost two Super Bowls to the 49ers, participated in the event and was amazed at the turnout of 30,000 fans.

"To hear the fans go crazy and see the admiration from these former players like Ronnie Lott and Joe Montana, that to me was impressive," he said.

A month later, the 49ers played their first home game at Levi's Stadium in Santa Clara.

***

There is a page in the 49ers' media guide dedicated to the team's winning tradition. Neither Eddie DeBartolo nor Bill Walsh, the owner and head coach who had started the tradition with that unexpected first Super Bowl team following the 1981 season, is mentioned.

CHAPTER 12

THE TERRIBLE YEARS

BILL WALSH KNEW he was dying. His youngest son, Steve, had died of leukemia, the same disease that challenged him now to climb the 26 steps to his second-floor office in the Arrillaga Sports Center on the Stanford University campus. There was an elevator, but Walsh refused to use it.

"Some days I feel invigorated," Walsh had said. "Other days I can't even go up these stairs. Oh, I *can* go up, but I don't want anybody to see me, because I'm holding on for dear life to get up those stairs."

Only his closest friends knew of Walsh's three-year struggle to live. Others believed they knew, but didn't want to believe their private thoughts.

On another weary day in the spring of 2007, the kind that made sitting a joy, Walsh called his secretary, Jane Walsh (no relation). "This is Bill," he said. "I'm over at the Stanford Hospital. I need you to get ready. I've probably, maybe got two weeks to live. Now, don't get emotional. There are guys I want you to call. Just write these players' names down."

Walsh then recited the names of a dozen players who had been with him during the glory years of the San Francisco 49ers. Walsh had coached them in his unique way, using a boxer's speed as a teaching tool and quoting famous military commanders to motivate his troops. He quickly turned a slow, beaten team into a dynasty that won four Super Bowls in the 1980s. "The good, old days, the days of Camelot," former 49ers executive John McVay called the exciting decade.

But now Walsh was calling out the names of his stars with a purpose that had nothing to do with winning games. He wanted them to be among the first to know that his struggle with leukemia was about to end.

"He wanted to meet them and share old stories and laugh at his humor," said 49ers owner Eddie DeBartolo, Jr. "He wanted to say goodbye and tell them how much he loved them."

Six months earlier, Walsh had talked in private about planning his funeral. Jane Walsh, his secretary, listened with tears in her eyes as she wrote in a notebook the details of the service. Walsh had it all planned. The music. The homily. The main eulogy. The names of six of his closest friends who would reflect on his remarkable life.

Walsh wanted the service to include a bridge to his old team, even though he no longer attended 49ers home games. The speakers would include Joe Montana and Steve Young, Walsh's two best quarterbacks, his old friend Mike White, his highly competitive team owner Eddie DeBartolo, Jr., National Football League Commissioner Roger Goodell, and United States Senator Dianne Feinstein, a friend from her years as mayor of San Francisco. Dr. Harry Edwards, a sociologist hired by Walsh to provide stability to his younger players, would give the eulogy.

Walsh wanted the service to be uplifting to his guests. If he had his wish, there would be no recognition of his accomplishments, only the celebration that he was a good man, a purposeful man, who had made a difference in other peoples' lives.

The 90-minute service, "A Celebration of Life for Bill Walsh," would be held in the historic Stanford Memorial Church. The church is the spiritual home of religious life and the centerpiece of the main quad. The façade of the inter-denominational chapel, built in the early 1900s, features 20,000 shades of color and gold leaf in the tiles.

Nearly every part of the church is decorated with carved stone, polished wood, glowing stained glass, or Venetian glass mosaics. The church was built by Jane Stanford in memory of her husband, Leland Stanford, Sr., who with her had founded the university that bears their name in Palo Alto.

It seemed only fitting that Walsh would chose to be eulogized on the campus where he coached (1977–'78 and 1992–'94).

"At this stage of my life," he said, "I feel closer to Stanford [than the 49ers]. When I came here, it was just a perfect move for me. I feel very comfortable here, and I think they [the 49ers] are comfortable without me, to be honest with you."

More than 1,200 mourners from Walsh's world of players and friends would be invited to attend the celebration. Jane, his secretary of 18 years, wept for four hours in his office after Walsh had finished with his plan. She refused to leave and show her tears until dusk had covered the Stanford campus

"He sort of orchestrated everything," said Mike White, who coached under Walsh with the 49ers and at Stanford. "He made such an effort to say goodbye to everyone in his own way. I drove down from a summer camp one time, and Joe [Montana] was there, Ronnie Lott, too. Then Eddie [49ers owner Eddie DeBartolo, Jr.] came by. It was amazing the way he did it with such dignity. There's no telling how he felt, but he made you think things were going good. He just wanted to look you in the eye one last time and see what was going on. I don't know, there's never been one like him."

Walsh had always been a man of detail. As a teenager, he'd worked weekends for his father, Bill, who owned a small body-and-fender business outside of Los Angeles.

"I would sand the cars and prepare them for painting," Walsh once recalled. "I would assist him all day, and when the day was over, he'd give me a dollar."

Craig Walsh, the coach's oldest son, often talked to his father about the postwar boom of the 1940s and 1950s.

"He was a real blue-collar kid," said Craig Walsh. "My grandfather painted cars in his spare time job. My dad would help him with the projects. He wanted my dad to get into the custom car-painting business because it was just taking off."

It was a time of cruising along downtown streets with flashy hot-rods. Bill Walsh got caught up in the trend and the jazzy colors of the cars that thundered along the streets of Los Angeles. "He loved sanding cars and painting them," said Craig Walsh. "It was a kind of hobby back then."

It was also dull, tedious work. Yet, Bill Walsh never complained about rubbing down cars.

"You learned a few details, because that was the kind of business it was," he said. "That was what was expected of me. So my dad gave me a work ethic, whether he meant to or not."

Walsh's father, a man who had decent athletic skills but rarely competed because of the family demands during the Great Depression, completed only the eighth grade. His mother dropped out of school after her junior year. Nevertheless, Walsh would take from his parents a sense of pride and equal opportunity and the importance of self-motivation. They taught him the simplest of equations: hard, productive work equals success. Later, in the sport that defined his life, Walsh and the 240 players he coached during his 49er years would succeed through the Walsh family doctrine.

In his third season as head coach of the 49ers, Walsh emerged as "The Genius." The accolade originated in media circles after Walsh's nervy and youthful team upset Cincinnati 26–21 in Super Bowl XVI. Walsh had used two obscure backs named Ricky Patton and Earl Cooper. Patton and Cooper were ranked thirty-fifth and fifty-fourth among National Football League rushers, but they were capable pass catchers and hard workers and fit into Walsh's quick, rhythmic system that came to be known as the West Coast offense.

Walsh could never shake The Genius label.

"It was flattering," he admitted. "But I was alert enough to it to know that it could come up and bite me real quick."

After his death from acute myelogenous leukemia on July 30, 2007, Walsh was eulogized 10 days later with the distinction, as they again called him The Genius. But this time the term was more serious and far-reaching.

"I thought Bill was one of the head coaches who was technically brilliant," said former NFL coach Dick Vermeil, whose early career linked him with Walsh. "But he could also see the big picture of the whole organization and the whole scheme of things. And he put it together as a leader and then coached it as a leader, probably better than anybody has ever done it."

Some rival coaches had mocked the genius label, claiming Walsh's teams lacked physical toughness—a "finesse team" some of them called the 49ers. That term irked Walsh. But there was another side to the issue: Some teams believed all of those softie stories, only to discover that Walsh's teams actually loved a back alley fight. Then, in a 1981 road rumble in Pittsburgh won by the 49ers, strong safety Carlton Williamson knocked out two Steelers receivers, and that was the last of the finesse stories.

Actually, Walsh had always rated speed and quickness over muscle and girth. Indeed, as a former amateur boxer, he likened the game of football to a team of 11 boxers, all nimble and quick with their feet and hands.

"He always talked about boxing. If you could beat a man to the punch by that much, you win" said former quarterback Steve Young as he held his thumb and forefinger about an inch apart. "That's what we practiced for . . . that much of an edge. He was probably right."

Before Walsh died at his farm-style home not far from the Stanford campus, he had answered all the questions that run through the minds of mourners. Walsh, it seems, always had the persuasive answers. Indeed, Eddie DeBartolo sensed that his brilliant coach had prepared for his death as if it was another Super Bowl.

"He was an unusual man," said DeBartolo. "There's no way I could do it the way he did it. He died with class and dignity. That's the way

Bill Walsh coming off the field after his final game, a Super Bowl win over Cincinnati.

he lived his life. It was just like he had scripted the first 15 offensive plays for a game. He scripted his death."

Scott Ostler, a fine writer for the *San Francisco Chronicle*, likened the success of Bill Walsh to a miner who discovered gold in the rush of 1849.

"They were wild, restless, desperate and a little bit crazy," wrote Ostler of the settlers. "And the spirit of those 49ers may have seen its last spark in a gray-haired football coach who struck gold without getting his hands dirty. Walsh's story is the last great gold-rush saga."

Ostler likened the 49ers' Super Bowl years to "an amazing machine and all he [Walsh] did was select the parts, assemble them by his own blueprint, teach, coach, inspire, and lead." Added Steve Young, "The man who brought it all together."

In the final year of his life, Walsh reduced his hours of play at the Sharon Hills Country Club course. On his best days, he would play as few as five holes in the morning sun. When fatigue left him too weak to even reach the first hole, he quit the game forever.

He stopped playing tennis, too. Walsh was a left-hander with a big service and a clever game. He loved the sport, probably because it involved quick, instinctive movement, the basis for his West Coast offense. He played rousing doubles matches on the courts owned by Woodside neighbor Paul "Red" Fay, Jr., a close friend. Fay was a Navy buddy of President John F. Kennedy. They remained friends after World War II, and Fay served as an usher at Kennedy's marriage to Jacqueline Bouvier in 1953.

Although Fay was a Republican, he was appointed Under Secretary of the Navy by Kennedy, who liked his engaging personality and business acumen. After Kennedy was assassinated, Fay moved back to California, where he met Walsh. They shared a passion for tennis and began socializing and playing on a regular basis.

Walsh loved playing at the NFL's annual winter meetings held at Waikiki Beach, Palm Springs, and Phoenix. It was always tennis weather, warm and bright and invigorating. Walsh usually played in the early morning sun with his football friends, Jim Finks and Eddie LeBaron, former pro quarterbacks who became successful football executives.

"We were about evenly matched," said Walsh. "We had some fun on those courts. Back home, I used to play three days a week. But I had to stop after the diagnosis. I started taking spills on the courts. There's probably nothing worse than falling on an asphalt court."

John McVay, Walsh's top executive during the 49ers' big years, remembered a tennis incident that reflected Walsh's passion for the game. The 49ers trained at Sierra College in Rocklin, California, about 25 miles northeast of Sacramento.

"Every now and then in camp he'd get the bug—he'd want to play tennis," said McVay. "One of the guys who worked at the college agreed to have a tennis match with him. And the dumb s—t beat Bill, which caused all of us much pain and suffering. The next couple of days he was in a foul mood." Walsh lengthened the team meetings a half-hour. His practices were grim and hard without the usual defense-offense cross-line banter.

Mike White, Walsh's former assistant coach and friend, ran a summer camp near the Sonora Pass, west of Stockton. The elevation there climbs to more than 5,000 feet. The campers are graduates and friends of Cal-Berkeley, Stanford's heated college rival. They slept in tents and played relaxing games, far less serious than the games in Walsh's world. Walsh, an avid outdoorsman, visited White's camp in the summer of 2006, just a year before he died.

"When he was here, he was Bill Walsh the person, not Bill Walsh the Super Bowl man," said White. "He was in the middle of *everything*. He played softball with the other campers. He would be sitting in the dining hall, talking to people. I mean, they couldn't believe it. One time they made him wear a Cal hat and they took a picture. It was in our next brochure. It didn't bother him. That was part of him from the very start of our relationship. When he got out of the limelight and away from the day-to-day routine, he had an unbelievable sense of humor."

During his three-year ordeal with cancer, Walsh refused to dwell on his poor health. He was stoic about his disease, about the injections and transfusions and a depressing 11-day stretch in the hospital with pneumonia. Anyone who has ever undergone a bone marrow biopsy knows what Walsh went through in the exploratory stage of his illness. A special biopsy needle is inserted near the hip area and eased downward until it reaches the bone. The needle is used to remove the marrow cells, which are then examined under a microscope. Presumably, in Walsh's case, many of the normal marrow cells had been replaced by abnormal cells known as leukemic blasts.

According to the Leukemia & Lymphoma Society, this condition leads to a deficiency of red cells. These normally healthy cells are "filled with hemoglobin, the protein that picks up oxygen in the lungs and delivers oxygen to the cells all around the body." Without sufficient red cells, the patient is left anemic and susceptible to infection. In 2007, the year that Walsh died, 13,410 new cases of ACL were diagnosed, most of them in individuals over 65. "Old man's leukemia," Walsh's lawyer, Steven Kay, had called it. Walsh was 75 when he died.

Walsh had undergone two back operations. His first operation in 1991 was similar to the surgery that Joe Montana needed in 1986 for a ruptured disc in his back. Nine years later, Walsh underwent a much more serious back operation that lasted more than five hours.

"My nerves were wrapped all around my spine," Walsh said. "They had to clear that out. Cut part of the spine away. They had to take three vertebrae and rearrange everything. Oh, God, it was painful."

Walsh began rehabilitation at a therapy center. He was making progress, but soon was unable to do any of the stretching or bending routines designed to restore normal back functions.

"I lost all my energy," he said. "It was painful when I did anything, like just walking. It was ridiculous. I'd have to find a place to sit down at a moment's notice. The greatest feeling of all was when I finally got to sit down at home and just be there, maybe fall asleep or something."

As his condition worsened, his personal physician, Dr. Michael Jacobs, wanted to perform a series of tests on Walsh. The coach, perhaps thinking that his condition somehow related to his earlier back surgery, kept skipping appointments.

Walsh, now without his appetite and the energy of his youth, finally agreed to be evaluated. What the doctors found was a condition known as myelodysplastic syndromes, or MDS as Walsh knew it. The term has been used to describe a group of diseases of the blood and bone marrow that produces millions of white and red cells and platelets. The presence of MDS reduces the number of healthy cells and platelets, leaving the patient feeling much older than their age. Walsh once went two weeks without eating a decent meal, his only source of food a few crackers.

"It got so that I didn't care whether I made it or not," he once told me. "I was so darn sick."

Over those depressing days, Walsh kept his failing health out of the news. "I'm a little bit under the weather," he would tell friends. Once, when a reporter called his secretary to ask about seeing the coach with a bandage on his arm, she had a ready answer. "So what?" said Jane Walsh. "We all get polio shots." She later confessed about an order from her boss. "I had to lie, lie, lie, lie," she said.

Aside from being sick, Walsh had to care for his wife, Geri, who in 1999 had suffered two debilitating strokes that paralyzed her left side. Geri had been a superb athlete at San Jose State. Her best sports were tennis and golf, the same games that Bill loved so much. And, like her husband, those games had been taken away from her when she was 65. She shuffled along, cane in hand, to cover short distances. Otherwise, she moved around in a wheelchair.

"They had a caregiver for her, say from eight o'clock in the morning until 2:00 p.m., then another from two o'clock until six or eight o'clock," said Mike White, one of Walsh's closest friends. "And then Bill came on. He was the caregiver at night. The third-shift caregiver. He loved her dearly and talked about her all the time. But I knew it was sapping his strength."

Geri Nardini in her youth was an outstanding tennis and golf player. She attracted Bill Walsh with her dark, good looks and athleticism in the very sports he loved.

"She was from another high school," Walsh recalled. "She was beautiful. She was the best-looking girl in school. She was going on to college at San Jose State. I lusted after her, so that was as good a reason as any for me to go to the same school."

"I was registering for courses at San Jose State and he was ogling me," said Geri. "He was ogling *all* the girls. He was an upperclassman and I was a freshman. He asked for my phone number, but I didn't have a phone yet. So he asked me to come to a boxing match with him. He was fighting in the Golden Gloves, so I went to the arena to see him box. He won. I remember how wonderful he looked."

They married in 1956, after Walsh graduated from San Jose State and took his first coaching job at Washington High in nearby Fremont.

Walsh's salary was $4,650 a year. He had three assistants, all of them full-time teachers.

Thus began a long, climb up the coaching ladder, and Geri was by his side. They played tennis and golf together when Walsh wasn't coaching and trying to inspire 160-pound kids to run like sprinters and throw their bodies around. Over their years together, some of them agonizing years, Geri became his rock.

During those magical seasons with the 49ers, his snappy West Coast offense dominated the league and he became "The Genius" for winning three Super Bowls. But then his career took a turn downwards, professionally and personally.

Walsh had returned from a fling with television to coach at Stanford. But, after three years, two of them losing seasons when his defense couldn't stop anybody (allowing an average of 34 points in the 4–7 and 3–7–1 seasons), Walsh quit.

Two years later, Walsh was lured back to the 49ers front office as a consultant. It was a mistake for both parties. Even with John McVay again beside him as a confidante and adviser, Walsh couldn't recapture the glory years. There was a tricky salary cap in place that he had never faced. There always seemed to be suspicion in the air whenever Walsh was in the same room with the head coach, first with George Seifert, to whom in 1989 he had turned over "the best team in football history," and later with Steve Mariucci, an offensive whiz who once coached Brett Favre. More significantly, big spender Eddie DeBartolo was forced out as the team owner after a family feud and a casino gambling scandal. The new, conservative owners were Denise DeBartolo York, Eddie's sister, and her husband John York, who emerged from the DeBartolo corporate world.

Walsh had neither the energy, nor another Joe Montana nor the money, to build another championship team. Soon he made "the perfect move for me," and returned to the Stanford athletic department.

He stopped going to 49ers home games. Instead, each morning he entered his office in the Arrillaga Sports Center where there were three things on his mind: the university's failing football program, his former 49ers players, and Geri, the "darling" of his daily phone calls.

The couple had moved to Geri's dream residence, an old, abandoned Adobe farm house built in 1929. Behind the home was a two-acre vineyard, which thrilled Walsh.

"She took this house which had been deserted and never lived in for 30 years and totally modernized it," said Walsh. "Big windows. Skylights. She made it totally different. Now we still have a lot of the original window coverings, a lot of the old trappings and a lot of the new. It cost a helluva lot to keep it up because it's on four acres. Two acres of which are mine."

By the discrepancy in the acreage, Walsh, of course, meant the vineyard. A chardonnay man all the way, he'd begun a small winery behind his magnificent home.

"There was a little company that bottled his wine and sold it," said his secretary, Jane Walsh. "The home was beautiful. It looked like it was right out of *Architectural Digest*. I mean, *immaculate*. You know, sculptures and paintings. She loved art, and she herself painted."

Bill and Geri Walsh seemed to have it all. An enormous home in suburban Woodside tucked away off the 280 Freeway. A weekend beachside home in Pacific Grove on the tip of the Monterey Peninsula. Enough money from Walsh's coaching days and a three-year contract as an analyst with NBC-TV to live the good life. Yet, after her strokes in 1999, Geri couldn't enjoy the travel, the dinners in fine restaurants, the long walks along the beaches on the Monterey Peninsula or, of course, her two favorite sports, golf and tennis.

"It's been a sad, sad experience," Walsh told me. "Even today, just to see her. She will walk with a cane . . . . There are braces up and down her left leg to hold it straight. Her left arm doesn't function, either. She still goes to therapy for the good arm and the other leg."

Walsh recalled his wife's first stroke, saying, "One day her arm went dead," he said. "She called me and I rushed down to see her. I took her to the [Stanford] hospital and they caught it. I had dinner at a little restaurant near the hospital. They came and got me and told me she had suffered another one [stroke]. Fortunately, it was just in the arm. Then, three hours later, she suffers another one and a blood clot hits her brain."

Every time he reflected on Geri's tragedy, Walsh assessed blame. He blamed her doctors for not giving her a blood thinner like Coumadin that might have avoided her second stroke. He blames himself for not seeking a second opinion.

"I took her to the emergency room a couple of times," Walsh said. "She still looked so good that I think the doctor was fooled. But she was getting worse. I took her to the emergency room once in Hong Kong, after she had fainted on the plane. All of these things happened because of this, the failings and everything."

In 2004, five years after Geri's series of strokes, Walsh began suffering from fatigue. He was a big man, active on the tennis courts and golf courses. He also belonged to the Bohemian Club, a group that enjoyed camping outdoors in Northern California. One summer, Walsh had to stop midway up a lengthy hill to rest while the other campers went on. Every day after that jolting experience, he felt his energy level drop. He coughed frequently and often looked as if he had been up all night. What really bothered him were the endless tests and subsequent blood transfusions whenever there was a decrease in his red cells and the oxygen they carried.

When he was asked to describe a typical day, Walsh took about a minute to reply. "I get up late," he eventually said. "I get to the office about 9:30 and do some work. Then I go to lunch with someone. There are some personal things to do and some business here at Stanford. In the afternoon, there are sometimes some hospital visits going on. Then I go home fairly early and that's it."

As his condition worsened, Walsh wanted to make sure his players and his world of friends knew how much he loved them. Grown men, now more important than ever to the dying coach, began joining him at lunch to tell stories and be told stories by their special friend.

Many of Walsh's lunch partners were his former players. Walsh engaged them, got them to forget about sadness and his own hard times with stories of other, better years. Walsh often joked about his terrible illness. He spun stories with funny lines, because he didn't want anyone feeling sorry for him. Instead, he wanted to share the times and tell his lunch partners of his inner feelings.

"You know, a coach isn't your friend," said Steve Young, one of Walsh's Hall of Fame quarterbacks. "But because he didn't take on any regular duties the last while, it really gave him opportunities for sublime time together. Honestly, my feeling for Bill deepened in the last couple of years."

There were lunches at the clubby Sharon Heights Golf and Country Club and numerous downtown restaurants. Occasionally, Walsh would dine with a friend at Hobee's, a casual off-campus restaurant whose motto was "Fast, Fresh & Friendly." Hobee's was founded in 1974, a few years before Walsh began his head coaching career at Stanford. He was immediately recognized by the waitresses, who often asked for his autograph.

"Whenever Bill would enter a restaurant, the other diners would stand up and cheer," said Steve Kay, Walsh's lawyer.

As Walsh neared death, his former players began to realize the part that he had played in all of their lives.

Joe Montana, who played the game like an artist stroking a 100-yard canvas for Walsh, remembered the last time they met. It was three days before Walsh died. The coach appeared weak, almost helpless. Yet, he had a message for Montana to convey to his world of friends when the time for his service came.

"He wanted all of you to know that he loved you," Montana told the mourners on one of those sun-splashed days on the Stanford campus. Montana grew misty-eyed and needed time to compose himself. His final poignant line moved the congregation.

"Coach," said Montana, "we love you, too."

Eddie DeBartolo, the hard-driving owner who sometimes feuded with Walsh, had put their cold war behind him. He was now focused on how much Bill Walsh had meant to the 49ers and San Francisco, a city of cultural differences and ideological debate.

"He always told me, 'I love you,'" said DeBartolo. "He was coaching us. He was making us stronger and more prepared" for the final day in his life.

Walsh had not only transformed a team that had won seven games and averaged 12.3 points per game in two years, he'd brought sense to a city on the brink of collapse. In 1979, the year Walsh was hired to rebuild the hapless 49ers, San Francisco was a city of unrest. Mayor George Moscone and Supervisor Harvey Milk had been assassinated. There was a sense of disaster after reports of a crippling new virus known as AIDS. More shocking was the news that 600 Californians had died in the Jonestown massacre.

Senator Feinstein, the mayor when the 49ers won their first Super Bowl on January 24, 1982, said the championship changed the mood of a city that was in "deep despair." Hurriedly, her office organized a victory parade. The crowds packed Market Street, standing three and four deep to catch a glimpse of their new heroes. Montana and Lott. Keena Turner and Jack "Hacksaw" Reynolds. Dwight Clark and Randy Cross. Charle Young and Keith Fahnhorst. Freddie Solomon and Ricky Patton . . . .

And, of course, there was Bill Walsh, taller than the Golden Gate Bridge, beaming in response to the cheers. And Diane Feinstein, smiling to the faces in the crowd on the proudest day of her term.

"I didn't know who would come," she was to say at the celebration of Bill Walsh's life 25 years later. "But when we headed up Market Street, there were people hanging from the lampposts to see us."

There would be other giddy Super Bowl parades and a different cast of 49ers to follow, four more, to be exact. Yet, none of them would ever match the first one, the one that made San Franciscans glad that a very special man named Bill Walsh had become one of them.

Sadly, but perhaps understandably, Walsh chose to loosen his ties to the 49ers in his final years. Faced with a constant fatigue problem, he worked three and a half days per week in his office on the scenic Stanford campus. He played significant roles in two major football projects: modernizing the 85-year-old, 85,200-seat Stanford Stadium and hiring a new head coach.

Walsh campaigned for Jim Harbaugh when Stanford was searching for its next coach. This was a once-proud school with a history of star players, some of them legends. Yet, it had won only one game in 2006, the second-worst record in the 116-year history of Stanford football.

Harbaugh eventually got the job. Walsh was doubly proud because Harbaugh was a former pro quarterback who knew all about the West Coast offense.

Tired of seeing the aging stadium half-filled for home games, the school decided to drop its capacity to 50,500, offering better sightlines and facilities. Walsh was the catalyst for the project.

"Bill was the voice of Stanford, sort of the Stanford diplomat, if you will," said Dave Schinski, Stanford's assistant athletic director and director of capital planning and real estate. "You needed a trusted representative just to communicate the program. That's a big piece of what he did."

Over a dozen years, Schinski became a close campus friend to Walsh. "He wasn't just a coach," he said. "People say he was the mastermind of the West Coast offense, the most innovative, fantastic coach of his time. Absolutely he was. But he was also a philosopher of sorts in terms of cultural equity. He was sort of a human rights guy. And he was involved with these youth programs, basically for underprivileged kids and the Job Corps stuff."

With Stanford as his base and his ailing wife, Geri, as his life-long love, Walsh drifted away from the 49ers. Eddie DeBartolo, the team's former owner and Walsh's sometimes critic, was 2,528 miles away, starting a new construction business in Tampa, Florida. Former club president Carmen Policy had left to join the expansion Cleveland Browns. John McVay, Walsh's closest football executive, had retired.

As Walsh neared death, his players were drawn to him by the love for the most unique man any of them will ever know. They were together again, as they were on those sweltering days of summer camp in Rocklin or on those frigid Sundays in Green Bay or Chicago.

Players age out of their athletic years. And when their old teams change owners, former players can feel like outsiders, as if their time had come and gone. The old 49ers, the ones who played for Walsh with the instincts of boxers and the nerve of militiamen, clung to their fading coach. They professed their love, each of them feeling as if he was losing his father. Inexplicably, that love seemed to create a divide: the Bill and Eddie years and the Denise and John years.

In the last days of Walsh's life, there were many sad goodbyes, so sad that they brought tears to eyes of his friends. One of them was former 49ers general manager John McVay, who had been at Walsh's side through all of the big years.

"We'd talk every week or so during his illness," said McVay. "One time I went down and we did a tape for NFL Films. Afterwards, we went across the street and had a glass of wine and talked about the good, old days. The days of Camelot."

In late July 2007, they met in his second-floor office at Stanford. Walsh was very sick, barely clinging to life. There would be no jokes on this emotional day.

"Well, I guess this is goodbye," said Walsh, his lips tightening. McVay became misty-eyed, trying not to believe what Walsh was telling him.

Four days later, Walsh died at his Woodside home with his family beside him. At his request, he was cremated.

"He didn't want any more fanfare than we had to have for him, for people to have to think about it," said Craig Walsh. "He demanded that he be cremated, and we followed his wishes."

"A Celebration of the Life of William Ernest Walsh" was held on Thursday, August 9, 2007. The speakers included Montana and Young, friend Mike White, Eddie DeBartolo, NFL Commissioner Roger Goodell, and US Senator Dianne Feinstein. Dr. Harry Edwards delivered the eulogy, as Walsh had asked.

Tenor Gary Wynbrandt sang Walsh's favorite song, *Danny Boy.* Linebacker Keena Turner and 49ers coach Mike Nolan read scriptures from the Bible. San Francisco's Glide Memorial Church choir provided a rousing series of gospel songs, with an interlude of organ music by Johann Sebastian Bach.

The eight-page program featured a photo of Walsh, a dozen tributes, Robert Frost's famous "The Road Not Taken:"

Two roads diverged in a yellow wood . . . and I—I took the one less traveled by, and that has made all the difference.

The final page included a photo of Walsh and DeBartolo and lines from poet Henry Wadsworth Longfellow:

The heights by great men reached and kept; were not obtained by sudden flight, but they, while their companions slept, were toiling upward in the night.

On that warm, sun-drenched August morning, 1,200 mourners, including the entire Stanford football team wearing their game jerseys, filled the famous chapel. Geri Walsh attended in a wheelchair. At least a dozen NFL head coaches attended the ceremony, including Don Shula, Mike Ditka, Dick Vermeil, Pete Carroll, John Madden, Ray Rhodes, Dennis Green, two former 49ers coaches, George Seifert and Steve Mariucci, and current coach Mike Nolan. Another head coach, Mike Holmgren, stood at the rear of the chapel, misty-eyed and saddened, as he listened to the celebration of Walsh's life.

A large black-and-white photo of Walsh was positioned on the altar, looking down on the mourners. The photo shows Walsh leaning against a column, his face reflecting a mood of contentment. Some mourners said it reflected the image of this beloved man that they would remember. Senator Feinstein recalled the emotions stirred by the parade that followed the 49ers' first Super Bowl win. "Bill Walsh was a legend for us," she said. "What he gave to his city was putting together a team that would and could and did."

Dwight Clark, the receiver, described the service as a "family reunion." Clark said that Walsh "not even being here, he somehow brought all of us together. Even though it's a sad time, it's awesome to be around all of these people and tell Bill Walsh stories over and over. I'd like to thank him for giving us this opportunity to visit with each other and share all of the great times we had with him."

Freddie Solomon kept hugging his teammates in a display that reflected how close the 49ers had been in the Walsh years. "I feel so much joy here today," he said. "This is my family, these are my people, and I love them. I truly do."

Center Jesse Sapolu recalled the phone call he received from Walsh. "'He called to tell you that he loves you," Sapolu's wife told her husband. Sapolu added, "When I found out he was ill, we must have spoken 100 words, and 50 of them were 'I love you.'"

Steve Young offered a moment of laughter for the congregation when he recalled his first meeting with Walsh after he'd joined the 49ers in a trade from the Buccaneers. "He said, 'I thought you were 6-foot-2?'" said Young. In one of his early games, Young made a mistake, then retreated to the sidelines, where he was greeted by the coach. "Can't you do it like Joe?" Young recalled Walsh telling him. "He was tough and exacting. He demanded perfection."

Joe Montana was the final speaker.

"I didn't want to repeat what the others said," Montana was later to say. "But they kept bringing up the subjects that I thought I would talk about. I had thought of talking about his accomplishments outside of football, but Dr. Edwards talked about that. I was going to talk about how he stressed the team, but Steve talked about that. So I thought I'd talk about his humor. He always had this sly sense of humor, and he

was still like that at the end. But when I got up there, I couldn't talk."
After a brief period of silence, Montana talked about how much Walsh
cared about every one of his players. "The last time I talked with Bill,
he said 'Just tell the players I loved them,'" said Montana. "So I'd just
like to say to my coach and friend, Bill, we all love you, too."

Dr. Harry Edwards, a tall man with the thick build of a tight end, stood before the mourners who had assembled at the historic Stanford Memorial Church. The façade of the chapel, built in 1929, featured 20,000 shades of color and gold leaf in the tiles. Nearly every part of the church is decorated with carved stone, polished wood, glowing stained glass or Venetian mosaics. The 1,200 mourners were gathered on a warm August afternoon to honor Bill Walsh, the coach who turned a dispirited San Francisco 49ers team into a Super Bowl winner. Indeed, a dynasty with all those Super Bowl trophies in the case and gleaming rings on the players' fingers.

But Dr. Edwards, the key speaker during the 90-minute "Celebration of Life for Bill Walsh," left Walsh's big wins for the sports media to chronicle. He was there, standing in the pulpit of the inter-denominational chapel, to honor the coach for his social contributions. Sure, Dr. Edwards would mention the championship seasons and the famous players. But the thrust of his eulogy would be about love and social change.

"It has been said the only true measure of a life well-lived is the positive and constructive impact of that life upon other lives," he said, "and that the only valid measure of that impact is the size of the hole left in our lives in the wake of that person passing.

"And so it is with the passing of Bill Walsh. The magnitude of the hole left in our lives and hearts is incalculable." Edwards referred to Walsh as "a genius of football organization and strategy" and whose accomplishments "reverberate down through the seasons and far beyond the sports arena."

CHAPTER 13

TWO WHO CAME

DURING THEIR SUPER Bowl dynasty years, the 49ers quickly built a reputation for remarkable drafts. For example, in the 1981 draft, the 49ers took three defensive backs, Ronnie Lott, Eric Wright, and Carlton Williamson. All three became Pro Bowlers and Lott became a Hall of Fame safety. But there was another source of talent: free agents. Linebacker Jack Reynolds and cornerback Deion Sanders are two prime examples.

***

Jack Reynolds had played 11 seasons with the Los Angeles Rams, chasing Dallas and Minnesota to the Super Bowl, but never winning it. He was an aging run-stopper at a time when NFL teams were throwing a lot more passes, meaning their defenses needed younger, agile linebackers.

So the Rams let Jack Reynolds go.

A 37-year-old run-stuffer who was listed at 6-foot-1, 232 pounds but was really 5-foot-11, he was a football-smart, workaholic-type of player who could be seen with game films under one arm, his playbook under the other. He took a film projector with him on road trips.

"This is my projector," he said. "George [Allen] told me when he drafted me in 1970 that you can learn so much from film. So I bought one in '71. It even has my name on it."

All that made him Bill Walsh's kind of player, and the 49ers signed him before the 1981 season. Hardly anybody called him by his first name. When he joined the 49ers, it was "Hacksaw" Reynolds all the way.

As the 49ers soon found out, Reynolds came to their games prepared for battle. He could be found in a quiet locker room three hours before kickoff, fully dressed in his uniform, an empty look in his face. When the 49ers played at home, Reynolds would drive up the freeway to Candlestick in full uniform, ready to play in what he called "an action game."

"If I cared about things like Pro Bowls and All-Star Teams, it would drive me nuts," he said. "I've gotta do my *own* thing. Besides, I never say much. Oh, I have feelings about that [lack of recognition], but it isn't right to put another guy down in the process, or blow your own horn. I don't want to get involved in any politics. I like people who let their actions do the talking. Talk is cheap."

Reynolds played four seasons with the 49ers, proving to be an inspirational hitter who fit Bill Walsh's idea of a perfect team player. In Super Bowl XVI, when the Cincinnati Bengals were threatening to take the lead in the fourth quarter, Reynolds led a swarm of 49ers to smother 252-pound back Pete Johnson a yard short of the end zone (Johnson had rushed for 1,077 yards and scored 12 touchdowns that season). Reynolds read the formation and figured correctly that Johnson was going to run to his right, rather than over Pro Bowl left tackle Anthony Munoz, which would have been the logical call. Something about what Reynolds saw on that old projector of his tipped him off.

***

Deion Sanders played five seasons in Atlanta, daring receivers to beat his crowding, bumping style and returning kicks with those long, racehorse strides. But Sanders, known as "Prime Time" was never a good fit. The Falcons had a drab 30–50 record in the years Sanders intercepted 24 passes, returned five kicks for touchdowns, and headed for the Pro Bowl three times. So, when the 49ers offered a one-year, $1.34 million contract in 1994, Sanders fled Atlanta.

He joined a team that had won 68 games during his Falcon years, one of them a crushing 55–10 win over Denver in Super Bowl XXIV Among other bidding teams, the New Orleans Saints offered Sanders a four-year, $17.1 million contract. What swayed Sanders to accept the smaller, shorter 49ers deal were the conditions. The 49ers guaranteed their contract. There were no guarantees with the Saints, and besides, the Saints were coming off an 8–8 season and played in the same division as the street-smart 49ers.

As it turned out, Sanders brought more than his football skills to the 49ers. Forget the cast of big names in San Francisco. Forget Steve Young's remarkable season—3,968 yards, 35 touchdowns passes, and a 70.3 passing percentage. And forget the revised defense. Prime Time brought a brash, new attitude to the 49ers, a team that soon liked to rumble in those throwback uniforms of another era and looked very much like it belonged in the NFC East, the league's most physical division. Sanders introduced the 49ers to the "Prime Time Strut." The other players picked it up. "Part of his package," Coach George Seifert liked to say.

In the Bill Walsh era, the 49ers had won Super Bowls with Joe Montana's rhythmic passing and an underrated, big-play defense. In Super Bowl XVI, Bill Walsh rotated nine down linemen, dominating the Cincinnati Bengals. The 49ers won two other Super Bowls by embarrassing routs. In those years, the San Francisco defenses looped and slanted a lot, using Fred Dean, and then Charles Haley, as speed rushers.

With Sanders among 10 Pro Bowlers, the 49ers reached Super Bowl XXIX by upsetting the Chicago Bears, 44–15, and old rival Dallas,

Free agent signing Deion Sanders, who brought pizzazz and defensive skills to the 49ers secondary.

38–28. During the season, the 49ers swept the Saints, 24–13 and 35–14. After Prime Time clinched the first 49ers win over the Saints, returning a last-minute interception 74 yards in the final minute, it touched off a war of words that had its origins back in the battle to sign Sanders.

"You know what all the screaming is about?" asked Carmen Policy, the 49ers' president. "There's a little sheet independent of the contract. They call it the 'Financial Summary Sheet,' just a convenience to the people at the league who input the computer."

On Policy's financial summary sheet for Sanders, however, are the details on a $5 million option year. The Saints didn't hear about any option year until Sanders strutted into San Francisco in mid-September.

"The problem was that it was never reported back to the clubs," said Saints' vice president Jim Miller. "The Management Council says they got a one-year form that didn't say anything about an option year."

Policy argued back. "Look, it's almost impossible to do," he said. "We'd have to have $3 million worth of room to exercise the option. And if we don't exercise it, he's a total free agent next year. See, the option was [designed] to affect his free agency, not to affect the financial package."

Miller and the Saints never bought what Policy and the 49ers were trying to sell.

"Take it to an extreme," said Miller. "Say Procter & Gamble wants to put Barry Sanders in their company [in Cincinnati]. Say he's going to be their poster boy. Does that mean the Bengals gain an unfair advantage? Deion keeps saying 'Don't worry, wait'll you see how much I'm going to get. I'm going to get mine.' Makes you wonder if there's a third parry involved.'"

Policy, however, said that Sanders wanted exposure, not any $17.1 million deal with a team that's a Super Bowl longshot.

"Two more Monday night games, a Sunday night game, Saturday afternoon games," Policy recited. "The Dallas game is pumped up to be one of the big games of the regular season."

Saints owner Tom Benson, who had damned the Sanders signing, fumed. "What kind of Mickey Mouse organization are they running out there?" he sputtered. The 49ers took that as an insult. Accordingly, after Sanders strutted into the end zone following his interception return, their band played the Mickey Mouse theme song.

"I fined him $100," quipped 49ers coach George Seifert. "He was supposed to start high-stepping at the 20-yard line, but he started at the 25. I'll pay the fine."

In the 1990s, Tom Benson's Saints had a brief run as a playoff team before plunging to the bottom of the NFC West. What hurt the Saints probably more than any other team was an auditor's letter telling NFL owners that all teams would operate under a salary cap in 1994.

The Saints had sent out one of the league's best defenses in the early '90s, holding opposing teams to 211 and 202 points in back-to-back seasons. In 1992, four Saints—Rickey Jackson, Vaughan Johnson, Sam Mills, and Pat Swillling—were selected to the Pro Bowl.

"We had four linebackers, and every one of them was a millionaire," said Benson, who chaired the NFL's Finance Committee. "And they were four great linebackers. That was ideal, rather than having a $1.5 million player and the rest $200,000 guys."

Later, the Saints were forced to match a $10.4 million offer made by the Washington Redskins to pass-rushing end Wayne Martin, a restricted free agent. Martin earned more than fellow line starters Jim Wilks and Frank Warren (and perhaps as much as the entire line group).

"I don't quite understand free agency," said Benson. "When we lost a big-name player, they jumped on our backs even though they regarded this as part of the American system. You know, you and I can do whatever we want after our contract expires."

Benson said he's seen millionaires and low-paid journeymen playing side-by-side without any sign of animosity.

"It's just being at the right time slot," the owner said. "It's a matter of timing."

Sure, back in the early cap years, it would have been difficult explaining the system to some graybeard team leaders who'd become a draft-day victim because of some high-priced rookie.

"It's going to be an adjustment year," Benson said, as teams started to deal with the salary cap issue. "It's not going to be easy for anybody."

Benson estimated his player costs in 1993, the year before the cap took effect, at $40 million, almost triple his first payroll of $13.8 million in 1985. The 49ers were winning all those Super Bowls in those non-cap years, with owner Eddie DeBartolo rewarding his top players with huge salary increases or bonuses.

The team accountants, who became known as "capologists," helped to keep the figures straight and legal. It was the coaches who had to deal with envy and greed, the evils of the NFL's free agency system.

How would the salary cap have affected the 49ers during their dynasty years? It would have been a tough call for some of the star players who would have had to choose between remaining with the 49ers family or leaving for another team offering a bigger paycheck.

CHAPTER 14

DWIGHT—THE CATCH IN "THE CATCH"

IT WAS GETTING late in the 1979 draft. The 49ers had already chosen James Owens, a running back from UCLA, with their first pick. The plan was to develop Owens, with his speed and shifty running style, as a wide receiver. If it worked out, Owens would be catching a lot of passes from Notre Dame quarterback Joe Montana, drafted in the third round.

When the tenth round began, some teams began drafting receivers with one idea in mind: to keep the legs of their veterans fresh through the hot, bruising days of summer. "Camp receivers," they were called. But, when Bill Walsh made wideout Dwight Clark his tenth-round choice, his idea had nothing to do with saving legs. Walsh recalled how the 6-foot-4 Clark had shown some ability during a trip to Clemson to scout quarterback Steve Fuller, saying, "He's a receiver who can catch balls in any situation, and in any kind of weather."

"Bill [Walsh] was going to Clemson to scout Fuller, and he asked me to get him a motel because I was from Pickens, which is about 15 miles from Clemson," recalled Sam Wyche, the 49ers quarterback coach. "Fuller had asked Dwight [Clark] to come along and be his receiver for the workout. I think they were roommates. When Bill came back, he said he thought Fuller had a chance to play in the NFL, but the kid that surprised him was Dwight Clark. Bill said he was smart, had good hands, and was just a shade under 6-foot-4. They drafted for 12 rounds back then, and we took him on the tenth round."

It didn't take long for Wyche to notice how Montana and Clark developed a special relationship.

"They bonded immediately," Wyche said. "They became roommates, and Dwight was the guy that Joe went to. *Everybody* liked Dwight. He was one of the most likeable players on the team."

So, how do you explain why Clark caught only 12 passes in his senior year and 33 passes total in his career at Clemson? Wyche wasn't sure of an answer. He only knew that Clark caught 525 passes for the 49ers, including "The Catch" against Dallas that sent the 49ers to their first Super Bowl win.

Dwight Clark, who made the most famous catch in 49ers history, before he passed away from ALS at age sixty-one.

"We used a progression system," Wyche said. "If there was a blitz and your first receiver was covered, you'd go to your second receiver. If he was covered, your third receiver should be open. It was a simple progression. We worked Joe in for a series, splitting time with Steve [DeBerg]. We did the same for Dwight. Four games into the season, he'd get three series, or 12 to 14 plays a game. By the end of the year, it was clear that Joe was going to take over. DeBerg had all the parts, but he was getting old."

Clark eventually became a starter, too, catching passes in bundles: 82 in his second year, then 85 in his third year, when he and Montana would combine for one of the greatest touchdown catches in pro football history. It became known simply as "The Catch," one of 554 catches that Clark would make in his remarkable nine-year career that featured two Super Bowls and two Pro Bowls. Owens, the first-round draft choice in 1979, caught 19 passes and was gone after three drab seasons.

While doubters, many of them from Texas, still insist that Montana was throwing the ball away and the 49ers just got lucky on Clark's touchdown catch that won a thrilling 28–27 playoff for the 49ers. Wyche knows better. Heavy rains fell in the Bay Area during the week before the 49ers' playoff with the Cowboys.

"We went down to Los Angeles and borrowed their practice facility for the week," said Wyche. "The play was called 'Sprint Right Option.' On Thursday afternoon that week, we practiced it five or six times. Joe's job was to get the ball to [Freddie] Solomon running in the flat. If Freddie didn't get open, Joe was to keep the ball alive. Joe threw it just in time to Dwight, who came down three yards from the end line. He had to jump and still come down in-bounds." (The defender was Everson Walls, who'd had a spectacular rookie year with 11 interceptions.)

By now, "The Catch" and all the other thrills that Dwight Clark provided have slipped into history. In late November, 2017, Clark was diagnosed with ALS (amyotrophic lateral sclerosis), also known as Lou Gehrig's Disease.

Clark wrote on the website of owner Eddie DeBartolo, Jr. that he started to feel a "weakness" in his hand in 2015. "I was mildly paying attention to it, because since my playing days I've constantly had pain in my neck. I was thinking it was related to some kind of nerve damage, because it would just come and go. After months of tests and treatment, I got some bad news." Clark had been diagnosed with ALS.

Jeb York, the 49ers' CEO, said the team was "fortunate to know him more intimately as a wonderful man who has given so much of himself as an ambassador to the entire Bay Area. We will stand alongside Dwight and his family as they wage this battle."

Clark suspects that his football career caused the disease and hopes that the NFL will work with the NFLPA to improve safety with regard to head injury.

Clark, who was sixty when he learned of the disease, said he lost significant strength in his right hand, midsection, and lower back and right leg. "I can't play golf or walk any distance, and picking up anything over 30 pounds is a chore," he said.

"Dwight has been an integral part of my family's life for decades," said DeBartolo in a statement. "We are absolutely devastated. We vow to do everything in our power to support Dwight and Kelly and help them fight this terrible disease."

Montana and receiver Jerry Rice were also shaken by the news of Clark's disease.

"This is a difficult time for Dwight, Kelly, and all of us who love him. He is family and in our continual thoughts and prayers," said Montana.

"D.C. has done so much for me as a player and friend," said Rice. "My rookie year he showed me how to run that 'out' route. We know him for The Catch, but he's a great individual who cares about people."

According to the ALS Association, "Every 90 minutes, someone in this country is diagnosed with ALS, and every 90 minutes another person loses the battle against this devastating disease." The ALS Association says the disease's first symptoms appear with twitching and weakness in an arm or leg. "The weakness in your muscles progresses until you lose your ability to move . . . to talk . . . to swallow."

As it turns out, Clark isn't the first 49er to be struck by the disease. According to an NFL Alumni newsletter, three members of the 1964 team were diagnosed with ALS, quarterback Bob Waters, Pro Bowl linebacker Matt Hazeltine, and fullback Gary Lewis. The victims left doctors puzzled and searching for answers. Indeed, Waters sent out questionnaires to 114 former teammates about their physical condition and any medications they may have taken. The study never reached any conclusions about the disease, which strikes one in 50,000 Americans but took down three athletes from the same team.

Near the end of the 2017 season, DeBartolo and the 49ers began holding a series of events for Clark. By then, the former hero of so many big games could hardly walk. He greeted his former coaches and teammates at luncheons from a wheelchair. There was a special Dwight Clark Day on November 22, when the 49ers played the rival Dallas Cowboys. Clark made sure all his former teammates and coaches from the 1981 Super Bowl team were invited. And guess who was there as a special guest? Everson Walls, the defender on Clark's famous catch, who came to pay his respects.

"Everybody was wearing Dwight Clark T-shirts," said 49ers former executive John McVay. "It was quite an event."

In a move that carried out the 49ers' family theme, Clark bought a ranch-style home in Kalispell, Montana, not far from where DeBartolo owns a ranch. DeBartolo has the goal post near which Clark made his famous catch in 1981 in the backyard of his ranch. The location isn't far from Glacier International Park.

"He wanted to get away from it all," said DeBartolo. "His wife is a rider, and they've got a couple of horses. It's sad, so sad that you can't do something about [the disease]. You feel helpless."

Dwight Clark died on June 4, 2018, fifteen months after being diagnosed with ALS. He was sixty-one years old.

"I lost my little brother and one of my best friends," DeBartolo said. "He was an expansion of my family."

CHAPTER 15

CATCH ME IF YOU CAN

THERE IS AN old sports adage about "snatching victory from the jaws of defeat." But if it didn't originate early in the 1987 NFL season, it certainly fit.

The 49ers were struggling in a road game against a Cincinnati team that would win only four matchups. With only a minute to play, the Bengals led 26–20 and needed only to run out the clock to win.

On fourth down, Bengals coach Sam Wyche took a delay-of-game penalty, leaving only six seconds on the clock. And then Wyche, a former 49ers assistant coach, disdained a punt and called for a power sweep, figuring it would be the last play of the game. But tackle Kevin Fagan stopped the play with a burst to the runner, giving the 49ers the ball at the Bengals' 25-yard line with two seconds to play.

Joe Montana led the offensive unit onto the field to execute the final play known as "76 Tandem Left All Go." The 49ers sent three receivers to the left side, while Jerry Rice lined up on the right. All four receivers would run deep "go" routes.

To Montana's surprise, the 49ers' best receiver drew single coverage. The star quarterback saw the chink in the Bengals' armor and lofted a high spiral to Rice in the end zone, tying the score. Ray Wersching's conversion gave the jubilant 49ers a 27–26 win, snatching it from the jaws of certain defeat.

Over his Hall of Fame career, Rice made many game-winning catches, but none as unexpected as that one. Eddie DeBartolo, who usually left the owner's box for the locker room with two minutes left, this time headed for his limo in the parking lot. He was called back, and his mood changed from anger to jubilant. The 49ers dressing room was filled with wild shouts of joy, back-slapping, and body-bumping.

"It was absolute *mania*," said Coach Bill Walsh. "Everybody was wild, screaming and jumping. You couldn't believe it. It went on and on, players screaming and hugging each other, lying on the floor and kicking the lockers."

"He [Montana] spotted me in favorable coverage," Rice was later to say. "He lofted a perfect throw my way. I jumped as high as I could and came down with the ball.

"I remember watching Bill Walsh literally skip across the field with excitement," said Rice. Many noticed Rice's composure in those last tense seconds.

"How was I able to keep calm in that situation? No matter how tense the situation, or what is at stake, you need a brief millisecond of distraction," he explained. "When I lined up on the line of scrimmage, as my heart pounded, I'd look into the stands or at a sign or at photographers on the sideline, anything that took me away from the moment at hand."

Jerry Rice, of course, was one of the best trades made in the history of the NFL draft. He became a Hall of Fame receiver and held most of the 49er career reception records, including points, (1,130), touchdowns (187), catches (1,281), and yards (18,247) in his 15 seasons with the 49ers.

Walsh, who'd pulled off that historic draft-day trade for Rice while the other clubs weren't looking, sometimes couldn't stop talking about this skilled athlete.

In his foreword to Jerry's autobiographical book *Go Long! The Journey Beyond the Game and Fame,* Walsh remembered the first day of the 49ers mini-camp in June 1985:

Most of our veterans and recent draft picks had gathered at our practice facility to begin preparing to defend our Super Bowl title. It didn't take very long on that first day of practice for players and coaches alike to stop and stare at the new kid on the block. A few even gave me an approving nod. A six-foot-two physical specimen, first-round draft pick Jerry Rice was so explosive at every step that I think we were all in shock. I knew right away that Jerry was destined for greatness.

Rice had been timed at the NFL combine in 4.68 seconds over 40 yards, which wasn't impressive. But Walsh saw his explosive speed *after* the catch and based his major trade on that asset. Here is what one scout said about Rice in his pre-draft evaluation:

Fine size; huge, soft hands; catches the ball extremely well; makes the tough grabs over the middle; strong runner; can throw the ball; has been incredibly productive. Negatives: lacks super speed; isn't an elusive runner; will have to adapt to a new system. Comments: Isn't a true burner but is an ultra-productive receiver who will make his presence felt as soon as he learns his pro team's offensive scheme.

Rice played for Mississippi Valley State, a small 1-AA school located in a tiny town called Itta Bena, population 2,208. He could have gone to a larger college, but he liked Coach Archie Cooley's offense, which featured passes on almost every down. "And they were the only school to send a coach to watch me play in person," said Rice. "Coach Cooley had heard about me through a network of black high school coaches, and he told me I would be unstoppable at MVS."

What would impress Cooley was Rice's work ethic, the same quality that would impress the 49ers later in his career. Rice had always been a driven person dating back to his younger days as a helper for his father, a bricklayer, something he recalled in his book:

We would be up at 5:00 a.m. and work until sundown, tough work. My brothers and I would be the supply chain for my father, who actually laid the brick and mortar onto the structure. Bricklaying isn't fun work but it earned us money, some of which I turned over to my parents to help pay for clothes and groceries.

The family lived in Crawford, Mississippi, population 655, and Rice had never been on an airplane until he was drafted by the 49ers.

"I left Crawford, Mississippi, for a long stomach-churning flight to San Francisco," Rice recalled in his Hall of Fame induction speech in 2010. "I was scared to death, but at the same time excited. Scared about surviving the flight. Excited like I am now because I knew I was joining a great team that had already won two Super Bowls. And, of course, we went on to win three more."

The work ethic that Rice developed made him a natural friend of running back Roger Craig when they were 49er teammates. He began training with Craig and a few other 49ers in San Carlos, south of San Francisco, over an place of incline known as "The Hill."

"Almost daily, we met for grueling workouts at 7:30 a.m.," said Rice. "Three times a week we would run up a two-and-a-half mile hill against the clock. The last 800 yards there was a steep incline to the finish. I was in such good condition from running the hill that there was little difference in my play from the start of the game until the final whistle."

In 2010, Eddie DeBartolo was the presenter for Rice's induction into the Hall of Fame.

"The day he stepped on our surface in Santa Clara, you could tell he was different," said DeBartolo. "He worked harder than anybody else that I have ever seen. And I think it all stems from his fear of failing. He had a work ethic that goes back to when he was a child. Even the way he wears his clothes to the way he acts, no one will ever come close to that. He is a perfectionist."

"When he first joined us, he was so focused on football, he didn't want to deal with anything else," said Carmen Policy. "We tried to teach him with dealing with the media, how to solve other issues. Just what it would take to do a credible job."

DeBartolo singled out a 1988 playoff game against the Bears played in Chicago where the game-time temperature was 26 degrees below zero.

"They figured these guys from San Francisco coming in here weren't going to be able to handle the cold weather," DeBartolo said. "On the

Receiver Jerry Rice was introduced by Eddie DeBartolo at his Hall of Fame ceremony.

third play of the game, Joe Montana threw a pass to Jerry Rice in double coverage on the right sideline. He raced 60 yards for a touchdown. That set the tone. We went on to win the Super Bowl against the Cincinnati Bengals. Jerry was named the Most Valuable Player. He became the face of the franchise."

DeBartolo also recalled a Monday night game against the Oakland Raiders in which Rice scored three touchdowns, breaking the career scoring record held by Jim Brown. It was just an unbelievable night," DeBartolo recalled. "Jerry's record is some 25 pages long. I mean, we could be here for hours going over Jerry Rice's records. To him, the record that means the most is his 208 touchdowns. No one will ever come close to that."

In 2001, there was a publication called *Legends* in which the top 50 most significant Bay Area sports figures of the 20th century were rated. Oakland Raiders owner Al Davis topped the list. Jerry Rice ranked No. 8 on the list, just below Joe Montana (No. 2) and Bill Walsh (No. 6) and finishing ahead of such notables as Joe DiMaggio

(No. 9); Rick Barry (No. 17), Dr. Harry Edwards (No. 48), and Steve Young (No. 49).

"Irrespective of position, Jerry could be the greatest football player of all time," said Bill Walsh.

"He has been dominant for so long, which is very difficult," said Hall of Fame receiver Paul Warfield. "When you become a known commodity, people set their defenses to stop you. But that has not mattered. What he has been able to do is phenomenal. His numbers put him ahead of everybody. His numbers are so far out of reach. Greatest of all time? Yes, I would have to say he's the best of all time."

"It's publicly, privately, loudly, quietly, every day, every way, I try to beat Jerry Rice," said Michael Irvin, the Hall of Fame receiver from Dallas, just before he retired. "It's this Sunday, last Sunday, 10 Sundays from now, 100 Sundays from yesterday. When I line up, I want to know, what did Jerry do?"

When he joined the 49ers, Rice began studying a number of top receivers: Lynn Swann, John Stallworth, Drew Pearson, Tony Hill, and Steve Largent. "Then, when I got here, we had Freddie Solomon and Dwight Clark," he said. "I like to think of myself as a combination of all those guys."

CHAPTER 16

PERSONAL MEMORIES

WHEN I INTERVIEWED Bill Walsh over four days, he had a serious blood disease known as MDS (myelodysplastic syndromes). But those daily sessions, interrupted only by lunch, were spirited and detailed. Walsh gave no indication that he was suffering from a fatal disease. Indeed, the coach was almost always in an engaging mood, willing to touch on any subject except the serious nature of his illness.

Bill Walsh was the most remarkable man I have ever met. He was always reaching out to help others, a caregiver to his players and friends, most of whom were unaware of his health problems. By this time, he was working for Stanford University in its athletic department. He had an office on the second floor of the Arrillaga Sports Center Office located in the middle of the scenic Stanford campus. Walsh would park his silver Mercedes in a handicapped spot and walk a short distance to his second-floor office. And when he wore his favorite sweater, Walsh made sure you knew the color was Cardinal red, not 49er red.

The big years of Super Bowls and parties were slipping into history. Walsh had drifted back to Stanford, where he'd coached before, after his retirement from the 49ers. He and owner Eddie DeBartolo Jr. had argued their differences, then settled back to await another 49ers season, another chance at extending the 49ers dynasty with another Super Bowl win.

"I think after the second Super Bowl, Eddie wanted to do it every year," Walsh told me. "And he was so competitive, so emotionally involved, that he wanted to win it every year, and it just wasn't acceptable, just wasn't practical. The toughest thing was when we'd lose a playoff game. He would really feel it. His entourage from Youngstown was heavily involved in the game one way or another, and it could very well be that they were betting on the games . . . on the spread."

Walsh recalled a game against the New Orleans Saints, when Montana and backup Jeff Kemp were both injured and third-stringer Mike Moroski was moved into the starting quarterback position. The 49ers suffered a drab 23–10 defeat in that 1986 game.

"Moroski wasn't playing that badly, but he threw an interception and we lost the game," said Walsh. "After that game, Eddie was beside himself. That's when we had words, I'd guess you'd say—briefly. It was a misunderstanding by both of us."

After the 49ers returned to San Francisco, Walsh received a call from the senior DeBartolo.

"He asked, 'What happened . . . . What's going on . . . How are you doing?'"

Walsh said the next weekend, Eddie threw a team party to try and erase the memory of the defeat after which he'd thrown a wooden stool, breaking the door to a soft drink machine. "Eddie and I were on the dance floor dancing with our wives," said Walsh of that weekend following the Saints loss. "So those things happen."

Walsh agonized over the next season in which the 49ers finished 13–2. (One game had been removed from the 1987 season roster because of a player strike.)

"We all understood it was going to be a rebuilding year," Walsh recalled. "It was not going to be a great season necessarily. The season *after* that was going to be our great one. But we started winning every game and became the odds-on favorite to win the Super Bowl."

The 49ers, however, suffered a 36–24 loss to Minnesota in the '87 division playoffs early in January 1988.

"Eddie was distraught," he said, "It was really a tough time for everybody. It was really tough." Still, as Walsh had predicted, the 49ers won their third Super Bowl the following season on Joe Montana's last-minute touchdown pass to John Taylor.

Each of the four days we met, Walsh would talk about Joe Montana, his pre-draft workout, how the 49ers tried to gauge how the early rounds would play out and whether there was any other team with a serious interest in Montana.

"Oh, yeah, among John McVay, Sam Wyche, and myself, we called every team to express our own interest," said Walsh. "We'd name five players and he might be one of them. But in every case, Joe was certainly not paramount. The best we could get was that one of the teams said, 'Well, around the fifth round we might look at him.'"

Walsh called Montana "the ultimate pick for what we did. We knew he could make spontaneous plays. He had a way to do that. But above and beyond that, it was really gratifying to see that he learned our system as a student of football. He studied it without much fanfare. He went home and studied the game plays, which were very extensive here, because we changed the formation virtually every week on plays we would run. We'd run a play, but we'd change the formation to keep people off-balance."

Montana's first start came in a 1980 game against Detroit. On his first play, Montana was supposed to throw to Charle Young, who was split out as a tight end.

"He was wide open," said Walsh. "Joe threw it over his head into the stands. *Twenty feet* over Charle's head. I think he played another series. Then I replaced him [Montana] with Steve DeBerg. But I knew Joe was going to settle down."

Another game that Walsh talked about was the comeback win over New Orleans in which the 49ers trailed at halftime, 35–7.

"You think it's going to be 70–14 with another half like that," he said. "We came out at halftime, and Joe did an incredible job and brought us all the way back. Then we won in overtime. After that game, you could afford to think, 'This is for real. We've got that element in place.' After that, it was primarily defense that we were concerned about."

Walsh liked to talk about the 49ers practices in which Montana was "poetry in motion." His snappy workouts lasted 90 minutes.

"We'd have practices where the ball never hit the ground," said Walsh. "He just wouldn't throw a bad ball."

In one passing drill, Walsh would stand in back of the pocket and call out which of the five receivers Montana would throw to and when. As Montana made his drop back, Walsh would call out "no . . . no . . . *yes!*" and Montana would throw to the third receiver. Other times it was "no . . . no . . . no . . . *yes!*," and the receiver would be the tight end or a back.

"We'd do that over and over and over," said Walsh. "People would see him do that, drop back and throw to his back, who would make 10 yards. They'd say, 'He must have eyes in the back of his head.'"

The 49ers also worked on what are called "busted" plays, where the receivers are downfield and Montana was scrambling.

"We'd drop him back before our formal practice with our receivers already downfield," said Walsh. "So he'd move and they'd move. We did everything in our power as coaches to build his game. But still, he was a great football player above and beyond that."

There was also Montana's toughness.

"How he could get knocked down and get up with his head clear, thinking of the next play and functioning," Walsh said. "I mean, there isn't anything like that in any other sport, where you take that kind of punishment and still have to function. You'll notice people in other sports, they just lay there and people help them up. A quarterback has to get right up on his feet and get going again. See, we had our foot on the throttle all the time."

Walsh also liked to talk about Steve Young, Montana's successor, Ken Anderson, Dan Fouts, and a little-known talent named Greg Cook.

Drafted as a first-rounder by Cincinnati in 1969, Cook played only one full season when he was sidelined by a severe shoulder injury. He tried a comeback four years later, but retired after one game. Cook had it all: size (6-4, 220 pounds), mobility, and a big arm. His career totaled 12 games.

The name Tom Brady came up in one of our quarterback discussions.

"Brady is a Hall of Famer," Walsh quickly said of the New England superstar. "He's a true superstar. But if you want to compare him to Montana, I'd take Joe, because he avoids the rush better and runs better." Walsh remembered when the 49ers held a rookie camp for all of the draft-eligible seniors. "Brady was there, "he recalled, "but our coaches for some reason didn't look at him."

One morning, Walsh suggested that Montana could have been a standout baseball player if he had elected to focus on that sport.

"He had real athletic frame," Walsh said. "He could have been a baseball player with that kind of frame. Or a basketball player. He wasn't heavily muscled—I could see that when I watched the film. That is an added plus when you're looking at a player. And the fact that he grew up in that part of Pennsylvania where there is competition, severe competition. And the weather, he played in all kinds of weather."

In watching Notre Dame game films of Montana, Walsh said he was often left puzzled by what he saw.

"There were games where he would come in late and do miraculous things," he said. "And you'd wonder why he came in so late. What was he doing on the sidelines? You had the feeling that he shared time with the fellow ahead of him who really *looked* like a quarterback. Maybe the coach went on looks, I don't know."

In reminiscing about those week-long interviews with Bill Walsh, the question lingers to be answered: Will there ever be another team quite like the 49ers of their dynasty years? Hypothetical issues like this one are part of sports lore covering every era, and sometimes there is no clear-cut answer. But in the case of this remarkable 49er dynasty, there will never be another team that comes close to it. Just remember, there will never be another innovative coach and talent judge quite like Bill Walsh, and there will never be another owner like Eddie D.

And think of emotional moments like the time when they hugged each other after Super Bowl XXIII and Bill Walsh told Sam Wyche, "I love you" and Wyche replied, "I love you, too." In 1978, Wyche was a backup quarterback with the Washington Redskins, when they played the San Diego Chargers in a preseason game in Tokyo. Walsh was on the Chargers' coaching staff.

"I went down early for breakfast one morning and he got on the elevator with me," said Wyche. "He said, 'Let's have a cup of tea.' We had our tea, and we must have stayed there for 30 to 35 minutes. At some point I started smiling, because I had picked up on something. I said, 'Bill, you got me here for a cup of tea, but you're interviewing me.'" He said, 'If I ever get a head coaching job, I'll call you.'

Wyche retired as a player and began applying for a coaching job with a number of North Carolina high schools.

"Two of the schools said I didn't have any experience and therefore I didn't qualify," said Wyche. "Within hours after I had opened their letters, Bill called and offered me a job with the 49ers. Bill and I had great chemistry. We were always saying 'I love you. I love you.' We were like brothers. We should have been twins."

Walsh once called veteran center Jesse Sapolu and told his wife, "Tell him I love him." And when Joe Montana met Walsh just weeks before he died, the coach said to his famous quarterback, "Tell all the players that I love them."

Montana recalled their final meeting at the end of Walsh's funeral service. "Coach, we love you, too," said Montana, the final speaker.

The 49ers of the Bill Walsh years were a family of gifted athletes. And isn't love the deepest sign of affection within the members of a family? That's what made the 49ers so special, so caring for each other. And that's why there will never be another pro football team with such heart and extension to one another. Walsh even referred to it when discussing his team. "When Joe Montana throws a pass, he's an extension

Bill Walsh and his 49ers players enjoyed a special kind of relationship.

of Randy Cross," Walsh would say. "When Ronnie Lott makes a tackle, he's an extension of Keena Turner."

I defer to Pro Bowl tackle Keith Fahnhorst to make my case.

"When Bill first came to the 49ers, it was real bad," said Fahnhorst, who passed away in 2018.

But then Walsh developed a coach-player relationship that was so special in those Super Bowl years, in no small part because it was based on one aspect: love.

"It was love. I think it was," said Fahnhorst. "We realized how big a part of it was love after it was all over . . . after we retired."

Fahnhorst faced serious health issues later on.

"One time I was on the radio, talking about needing an organ donation because I needed a kidney," he said. "I was in Minnesota and Bill called me. Somebody in the Bay Area had heard about my condition and called Bill, who raised his concern. He ended our conversation by saying, 'I love you, Keith.' I said, 'I love you, too.' It was something that we made sure we talked about, it was nothing fake. It was *genuine*."

DeBartolo was an owner who got as close to his players as he could without wedging into their huddles. He always met with them after games, often handing out towels—and occasionally tossing some object when the game hadn't gone the 49ers' way.

The 49ers traveled in oversized jets, usually L10-11 models with 250 seats, meaning there would be extra room for players to stretch out and relax. On at least one occasion, those L10-11s were all in use, so the 49ers flew in a 757. The meals were first-class. Each player had his own hotel room if he chose. And in those pre-salary cap years, the 49ers were heavy on salaries and bonuses, even to the backups.

How close was Eddie DeBartolo to his players?

"We were playing the Bears in Chicago, and Charles Haley got ejected from the game," the owner recalled. "I knew he'd be alone, so I went to the locker room to be with him. He saw me and said 'Hey, Mr. D., they ejected you, too?' I never got over Charles Haley [who jumped to Dallas as a free agent]. But a small part of me took pride in the fact that the best defensive player on the Cowboys team was a 49er."

CHAPTER 17

EDDIE IN THE HALL OF FAME

"**I THINK HE WAS** savoring every single moment," said Carmen Policy. "I think this was probably the greatest honor of his life."

Policy, the 49ers' attorney and executive, wasn't talking about any of the team's five Super Bowls. He was describing the reaction of Eddie DeBartolo Jr., his long-time friend from their Youngstown, Ohio, years together, to being elected to the Pro Football Hall of Fame.

"I have never seen him so ready to handle whatever comes up, and handle it in an appropriate and balanced way for such a long period of time when there was some real pressure imposed," said Policy. "He never got overly excited. His speech was *fantastic*."

DeBartolo had been on the fringes of the Hall of Fame a number of times. In his acceptance speech, he recalled visiting the site in Canton, Ohio, as a youth just a year after it opened.

"It had just two rooms then," he recalled. "But as I looked around at the names—George Halas, Art Rooney, Tim Mara—I thought it was one of the most amazing places on earth. It is beyond my wildest dreams that my name will now be alongside theirs."

Hundreds of DeBartolo's relatives and supporters will never forget the Friday night party that DeBartolo hosted to mark his induction.

DeBartolo invited 1,500 guests, and it seemed like they *all* decided to come.

"It could have been [for] a wedding or an international business mogul or a movie star," said Policy. "It was jammed, and there were personalities, celebrities, and people from every walk of life there. This was an amazing event. The only criticism said was that it was so crowded, so big, that it was impossible to get around and see everybody and sample everything."

In his 3,800-word induction speech, DeBartolo repeatedly referred to the 49ers as a family, molded just as he and Bill Walsh discussed at that historic 1979 meeting in San Francisco. There was a bond established that night that never broke, despite the highly emotional kind of game the 49ers played.

"I don't think I've ever been more proud of him than after that presentation," said Policy. "My appreciation was really heartfelt."

Eddie DeBartolo at his Hall of Fame induction ceremony.

Midway through his speech, DeBartolo cited all of the 49ers departments and offices for their contributions.

"I stand here today for the equipment managers and the groundskeepers and the laundry crew who worked so hard," DeBartolo said. "I stand here today for the executive assistants, the PR team, and the interns who work through the weekends. I stand here for the scouts and the bus drivers and the cooks and the schedulers and the hotdog vendors and the community reps who might never ever see their names in lights, but they are every bit as important to building a winning football franchise as the players we root for on Sunday."

Then he focused on the parade of remarkable players assembled by Bill Walsh during the dynasty years. The theme, again, was family values.

"If there is one secret to the success of the 49ers, it is this," he said. "We did not see players as simply players. We saw them as men. We saw them as sons, husbands, fathers, brothers, with families and responsibilities. We knew that if we helped make it possible for them to bring their whole selves to work, they would give us their all. That's why we welcomed mothers, wives, girlfriends, and children to the team, sent gifts to them on special occasions and celebrated with them on holidays. We weren't just a family on Sundays. We were a family every single day. *We were a family every single day.*"

At one point, DeBartolo reminisced about the 1979 draft that changed the history of the 49ers, when they selected quarterback Joe Montana.

"He came out the next day, and I looked at him and nearly fell over," DeBartolo said. "He was a kid. He had a big Fu Manchu mustache. He looked like he weighed about 170 pounds, He was listed at 6-foot-2, and he didn't look an inch past six feet. I said, 'Oh, dear God.' It turns out that this was just his secret identity, because when he got on the football field, Joe Montana turned into Superman."

DeBartolo also singled out wide receiver Freddie Solomon, who'd died of colon cancer. Solomon lived in Tampa, where the DeBartolo offices are located, and he and Eddie developed a special relationship.

"Freddie became one of my dearest and closest friends, and I loved him with all my heart," the owner said. "Until his very last breath, he dedicated himself to helping kids. I never met a man who cared so much about others."

DeBartolo mentioned the reunions he hosts for the 49ers.

"We get together every three or four months in Las Vegas or Los Angeles. There are 20 or 30 guys who come. Jerry [Rice], Joe [Montana], Roger [Craig] . . . . We go away for two or three days and shoot the breeze. We're like grumpy old men. They are like sons and brothers to me," he said. "Their significant others are like sisters and daughters. I can tell you what all of their kids are doing today. *That's* what I mean by family."

DeBartolo recalled that, in the final year of his life, Bill Walsh worked on a secret project.

"About a week after I was selected to be part of the Class of 2016, I received a package in the mail from Bill's son, Craig," the owner said. "It was a small 49ers helmet with Bill's autograph and a note Bill wrote that said, *I knew it was just a matter of time. Congratulations on your election. Love, Bill.*"

If there was one aspect of the game that bothered DeBartolo other than to end it with a smaller score, it was injuries.

"When my players got hurt, I used to leave the game, meet them in the locker room, or ride in the ambulance with them to the hospital," he said in his speech. "When Jeff Fuller lost the use of his arm making a tackle in 1989, I felt an obligation to make sure that he and his family were taken care of for the rest of their lives. Frankly, I think we could use a little bit more of that sense of family in the NFL today."

CHAPTER 18

SHUFFLING QUARTERBACKS AND COACHES

AFTER THEIR SUPER Bowl run, the 49ers were forced to deal with major changes, some of them mandatory, others voluntary. With the entire league operating on a salary cap and free agency system, and Denise DeBartolo York determined to show a profit like the other 31 owners, the 49ers were forced to play the same kind of game as their rivals.

Since the 2000 season, with the new ownership structure in place, the 49ers have employed five different head coaches. Ironically, the only successful one was dismissed after the 2014 season. Jim Harbaugh left under conflicting circumstances after posting a 49–22–1 record and taking the 49ers to three NFC playoffs and one Super Bowl, losing to Baltimore in a 34–31 squeaker in the 2012 postseason championship. The game was played in the New Orleans Superdome where the 49ers had staged so many dramatic rallies in other years. Harbaugh was dismissed after a disappointing 8–8 season in 2014 and was quickly hired by Michigan, a Big Ten power. The 49ers claimed it was a "mutual" parting.

The 49ers next named Jim Tomsula as their new coach at the start of the 2015 season, a controversial successor who was a longtime defensive line coach with only one season as a head coach in the defunct NFL Europe League. "Jim did a heckuva job here," said general manager Trent Baalke, "I think he's gone in his direction and we've gone in ours. I feel very good about the direction we're headed, and I'm sure he does as well."

Two years and two more head coaching changes later, Baalke himself would be out of a job, as well as Colin Kaepernick, the controversial and injured quarterback who had spent 10 weeks at an Arizona training facility working on mechanics with Hall of Fame quarterback Kurt Warner. Following a crushing 2015 season, Kaepernick needed off-season surgery on his left shoulder, left knee, and right thumb, and the 49ers needed better pass protectors and a quarterback who took risks with his body.

In 2016, the desperate 49ers tried another new coach, bringing in Chip Kelly, a man of new ideas and a fast-paced offense. It was the team's second head coach in two years. The hope was that Kelly and a then-healthy Kaepernick could produce an exciting, high-scoring offense. But, after a dismal 5–11 2015 season under Tomsula, followed by Kelly's 2–14 the next, it was time for the purge. Gone were Baalke, the general manager. Gone was Kelly, whose hurry-up offense had fizzled. Kaepernick refused to take a pay cut, thus nullifying a trade with Denver; he'd renegotiated his contract after taking the team to the Super Bowl in 2012, his first year as a starter for the team. That renegotiation included a $12,328,766 signing bonus and averaged $19 million over seven years.

"We haven't done much," said Baalke in 2016, citing the obvious. "We're a draft team that develops. That's what we are."

Everybody knew the 49ers needed offensive help. Yet their top pick in the 2014 draft was linebacker Jimmie Ward, and three of their top four picks in the 2015 draft were also for defense.

In 2017, following a 13-game losing streak under Chip Kelly, the 49ers brought aboard another new head coach, Kyle Shanahan.

"We've got a lot of work to do," said Shanahan, who was Atlanta's highly successful offensive coordinator. "We did take over a 2–14 team.

We don't feel all of the answers are here right now. We need to improve in every way possible, and we're going to do that."

John Lynch was named the team's new general manager. Lynch was a surprise pick, since he was a Pro Bowl safety who had started a successful television career

Shanahan made sure he gave himself time and purpose to rebuild a sagging franchise. He signed a six-year contract and serves as his own offensive coordinator. Mike McDaniel (running game) and Mike LaFleur (passing game) assist Shanahan as members of a 25-member staff that is filled with young, inexperienced assistants.

The lineup of quarterbacks who tried, but failed, to excite the 49er offense was just as long as the list of coaches: Kaepernick, Blaine Gabbert, Thad Lewis, Matt Barkley, C. J. Beathard, and Brian Hoyer. Just before the 2017 trade deadline, Shanahan swung a major quarterback deal with New England to get Jimmy Garoppolo, Tom Brady's backup. It was a strange trade in view of Brady's age (40), and the cost (a modest second-round draft pick). It took a few weeks before Garoppolo felt comfortable in Shanahan's balanced offense system that had averaged 33.8 points and 415.8 yards per game during his last year in Atlanta, but then Garoppolo moved in as the 49ers' seventh starter in three seasons and led the 49ers to five wins in a season-ending surge.

Displaying a nice touch and emerging as the team's new leader, Garoppolo quickly ended the 49ers' quarterback folly. Winning made the game fun and meaningful again for the team's players. At last there was the potential for a competitive team after all of those dreadful Sundays when the 49ers seemed beaten by halftime. And after five straight wins, around a once gloomy locker room was the feeling that Garoppolo had the potential for turning the 49ers into a true competitor in the NFC West. Yet, as former Dallas Coach Tom Landry used to say, potential is the heaviest burden of all.

"He's creative," said young receiver Marquise Goodwin of Shanahan. "He knows how to get guys in position to win and be successful. That's why his offense has been so productive in the past few years. He's a mastermind when it comes to these things. When you've got a play caller like Kyle, there's no telling what will happen play-to-play."

The 49ers sent out a young offense that finished a respectable twelfth in total yards (349.3 per game) in 2017. The unit included seven starters with five years of experience or less. Among them was rookie tight end George Kittle. The defense, which gave up 383 points and ranked twenty-fourth, is much younger. The unit included seven starters with five years of experience or less. Among them were three No. 1 draft picks: linemen Solomon Thomas (2017), DeForest Buckner (2016), and Arik Armstead (2015).

"We loved how we finished this year," said Shanahan after his first season. "I do believe our players have fought hard all year. I thought for the most part our team competed this year and has done everything I've asked them to do. You can tell the guys really enjoy it, made it a lot more fun coming to work. I think it will lead us into really looking forward to next year, too."

John McVay, the general manager during the 49ers' dynasty years, liked the way Shanahan and Lynch have meshed.

"I'm very impressed with what Shanahan has done," he said. "And also with the general manager's job with John Lynch. One of their big jobs is to get these young kids and bring them along. And I think they've done that. They've rung the bell."

McVay remembers meeting Kyle Shanahan when his father was the team's offensive coordinator in the early '90s.

"He was just a kid then," said McVay. "He was not very flippant. He seemed like he was very serious and had a clear path to what he wanted to do. Now he's an excellent play-caller, and he's not flamboyant."

The timing of the trade for Garoppolo surprised McVay.

"Yes, I guess I was," he said. "I was also elated. I'm just impressed with the ability of Kyle Shanahan and John Lynch to work together. John Lynch has taken non-football things off of Shanahan so he can concentrate on coaching the team."

So, how did the 49ers dig themselves into a hole so deep after reaching the Super Bowl following the 2012 season? Jim Harbaugh's version goes something like this:

"Management didn't want to spend the money or cede more control of the team over to me."

The 49ers could take a lesson from across the bay. The Oakland Raiders were a struggling team at the bottom of the AFC West when they decided to remake their roster. After clearing the out the aging veterans and finding their quarterback in the 2014 draft with second-rounder Derek Carr, the Raiders were back. They went from a 3–13 team in 2014 (including a 52–0 blowout loss to St. Louis), to a 12–4 playoff team in 2016. So a relatively fast turnaround *is* possible in the ever-shifting NFL, if you want to spend the money. That's the big question for the 49ers' ownership, which has been content to play a tight-fisted game of economics after those free-spending Super Bowl years.

The 49ers apparently believe that Jimmy Garoppolo is their established quarterback. He led a floundering team to five late-season wins to close out the 2017 season with hope. At least three of the victories, though, were tainted. They came against teams either far out of the playoffs or, in the case of the Los Angeles Rams, a team that elected to pack its lineup with backups. Perhaps, as veteran guard Randy Cross once said of the 49ers' surge, it will take one of those Montana-type comebacks by Garoppolo to kick-start their return to prominence.

In 1980, the 49ers came out flat and fell behind the New Orleans Saints, 35–7, at halftime.

"The Saints embarrassed us in the first half," said Cross. "They went past our locker room at halftime, whooping and laughing. Bill [Walsh] said, 'Hear that? They're laughing at you.' That lit a fire. We came out and hit a few plays, then scored a touchdown. Then another touchdown, and another."

The 49ers, behind Joe Montana, eventually won in overtime, 38–35.

"That was the day the 49ers became the 49ers," said Cross. "Most people think it was when we beat Dallas to win the NFC championship.

But I think the foundation for the dynasty was built that day against the Saints. The cement was still wet, but the foundation was there."

The current 49ers had some exciting Sundays like that under Jim Harbaugh. But owner Jed York cut the ties with Harbaugh after one too many debates over control. York then proceeded to hire and fire his next two coaches, Jim Tomsula and Chip Kelly, before he listened to some people who knew coaching talent and hired Kyle Shanahan.

"I knew we had some hard work ahead of us," said Shanahan. "But I feel very good about the future of this organization and where we're at. I think we will have lots of opportunities coming up with the salary cap and draft picks."

Coming into the 2018 season and boosted by the NFL's increase in the total cap from $167 million to $177.2 million, the 49ers have the third highest cap space in the league at more than $46 million (source: NFLtraderumors.com; update June 23, 2018). The 49ers selected five defensive rookies in their nine-pick draft, but the two top picks were offensive tackle Mike McGlinchey and wide receiver Dante Pettis, both taken to help Jimmy Garoppolo and the offense. Linebacker Fred Warner, the third-round pick, should upgrade the defense, which finished 24th in the league.

Four days after Super Bowl LII, the 49ers and Shanahan placed their future on the right arm of Garoppolo, rewarding him with a multi-year, $137.5 million contract extension. Garoppolo could have waited for some other big-number quarterbacks (Kirk Cousins, Drew Brees) to sign, but he liked the direction the 49ers were taking under Shanahan, a Bill Walsh-type of creative offensive thinker.

"I knew I wanted to be here," he said. "This team accepted me when I first got here. Then we had some success down the stretch. You could see the pieces falling into place."

Garoppolo had started only seven games during the 2017 season. But the 49ers saw enough of his quarterback skills to reward him with a huge contract. The deal was reminiscent of the Eddie DeBartolo years of free spending—and so unlike the conservative style of current owner Denise DeBartolo, Eddie's sister. The beauty and climate of San Francisco also appealed to Garoppolo. "We're a young and upcoming team, with a phenomenal coaching staff," he said, "It's an exciting time to be in the Bay Area."

In 1981, a year after finishing 6–10, the same record the 49ers achieved in 2017, Bill Walsh and Joe Montana, his second-year quarterback, won the team's first Super Bowl. In his first two seasons, Montana threw 43 touchdown passes, 31 more than Garoppolo. But whatever the stats, this is another of those coach-and-quarterback bindings: Garoppolo and Shanahan.

So, why did the Patriots deal their young, promising quarterback to the 49ers? Here is my theory: Because of Brady's suspension in 2016, Garoppolo gained valuable experience as a starter. His agent then approached the Patriots in the offseason and suggested they renegotiate Garoppolo's contract. Knowing that they would be unable to keep

Jimmy Garoppolo, the 49ers' current quarterback obtained in a trade with New England.

both quarterbacks under the NFL's salary cap (they had to deal Drew Bledsoe under similar circumstances in 1997), the Patriots swung a deal with the 49ers for a second-round draft pick. Why the 49ers? Because the Patriots didn't want Garoppolo playing with the New York Jets or Buffalo Bills in the same AFC East division. Garoppolo then won five games for the lowly 49ers, gaining additional leverage on his blockbuster contract.

Former 49ers executives Carmen Policy, who lives in California's Napa Valley wine country, and John McVay agree that the team is headed in a positive direction.

"I believe they have credibility in Shanahan and their efforts to rebuild the team," he said. "Everybody loves the new man [Garoppolo]. It appears as though he has all the talent to make him a winner. Plus, he has a resemblance to the quarterbacks of the past who won titles for us. When you see him play, it's reminiscent of those kinds of plays that we were used to seeing."

Policy said the 49ers were in no position to delay Garoppolo's signing.

"He won the hearts of everybody in the Bay Area," said Policy. "They had no choice but to sign him. If they *didn't* sign him, that would have been the death knoll, in my opinion, in their efforts to move forward. Now they're ready to go. They have a quarterback in everybody's minds. They have a new lease on life. Now they've got to fill in around him. And people in their division are starting to flip backwards. So, we're starting to smell opportunity here."

Lynch said the signing of Garoppolo was "a tremendous opportunity [that] fell into our laps. We were giving each other high fives and chest bumps. It's impressive to watch the guy throw the football. There are very few people in this world who can throw it like him." Lynch said Garoppolo earned his five-year, $137.5 million contract "and we were happy to do it."

CHAPTER 19

FINDING THE WINNING EDGE

BETWEEN COACHING THE 49ers, preparing for the draft, and caring for his ailing wife, Geri, Bill Walsh somehow found time to author a 524-page book, *Finding the Winning Edge*.

How did he accomplish this time-consuming feat? As in the game itself, Walsh had two skilled workaholics, Brian Billick and James Peterson, at his disposal. Billick, who played tight end at Brigham Young and worked with Walsh, said, "I was a graduate assistant working on my degree in journalism, and Bill hired me as an assistant PR guy. He wanted a former player who could relate to the players. So, for two years I was on his administrative staff."

Dr. Peterson is a sports medicine specialist who has authored 43 books. He previously served as a professor in the Department of Physical Education at West Point.

Walsh's book covers every aspect of the pro football game, including motivation, game-day strategy, player evaluation, financial strategy, and a primer on how every department should be run, e.g., if you're the equipment manager, check the weather forecast and don't forget the rain gear if we're heading for bad weather in Pittsburgh. Additionally, he offers ways to handle the tricky salary cap and how to strike it rich in the player draft. In other words, *Finding the Winning Edge* is a virtual handbook for any aspiring coach, college or pro.

In another insight, Walsh even approves of the way the Oakland Raiders kept their secrets in-house under Al Davis.

"The need for strict confidentiality concerning specific matters and circumstances within the organization is critical," said Walsh. "Surprisingly, many clubs fail to place a sufficient amount of emphasis on this factor. One organization that has addressed the issue in a serious way is the Oakland Raiders.

Walsh divided the book into five parts: Experiences and Values, The Organization, The People, The Game, and The Business. As former 49ers assistant coach Mike Holmgren put it, "To Bill's way of reasoning, no detail or situation is too unimportant to be overlooked." Holmgren recalled a practice in which Joe Montana threw a pass "slightly behind" Jerry Rice, a pass that Rice would catch "99 times out of 100." Walsh, however, approached Holmgren and explained "in great detail when a pass involving that route had to be thrown 12 inches in front of the receiver, not six inches behind him."

Billick, who served on the 49ers' administrative staff during their big years, tasted the thrill of his own Super Bowl win. He became an NFL head coach and led the Baltimore Ravens to victory in Super Bowl XXXV.

"Oh, gosh, there are so many things," said Billick, when asked about Walsh's coaching skills. "You ask 10 different people, and you might get 10 different answers. Certainly, it's going to come back to his abilities as a coach, his strategic ability, his sense of timing, the creation of the West Coast offense. But there are any number of people who will tell you it was his ability to evaluate talent. They'll tell you it was his ability to teach. Or it's his ability to communicate. There are so many different things that make him as great, probably, and as comprehensive a fully dimensional a coach as there is."

A perfectionist?

Hall of Famer Ronnie Lott celebrates another 49ers win.

"Oh, very much so," said Billick. "I go back to the old Don Shula line: 'What mistake is worth overlooking?' You know, he was not only a perfectionist, but he articulated very well. He was a control teacher. That's the number one thing I think of when I think of Bill Walsh. That he's the constant teacher."

Billick feels that Walsh was also a tough coach, a quality that is very much in evidence in *Finding the Winning Edge*.

"Tough, but only in the sense that he'd get to his players in a lot of different ways. He'd go after the coaches, rather than dress down a player on the field and call a player out. He'd challenge the coach in front of the player, trying to elicit a response from the player. He'd say to the running backs coach, 'Can you get him to punch with that right hand? Can you get him do that? 'Cause we've got no chance if we don't.'"

Finding the Winning Edge is packed with quotes from famous military commanders.

"He was very much a student of military history and recognized that the analogies of war have always been made to football," said Billick. "Bill was a voracious reader. He wanted to learn about men who were in the ultimate pressure situation and how they reacted. I particularly found that he was drawn to that individual who overcame his circumstance. Maybe he wasn't the commander in chief. Maybe he wasn't particularly gifted or the best warrior, but, when the circumstance presented itself, all if a sudden he arose and fulfilled that role."

A few examples of military leaders who impressed Walsh:

Discipline is based on pride in the profession of arms, on meticulous attention to details, and on mutual respect and confidence. Discipline must be a habit so ingrained that it is stronger than the excitement of battle or the fear of death.—General George S. Patton, Jr.

Duty is the simplest word in our language. Do your duty in all things. You cannot do more. You should never wish to do more.—General Robert E. Lee

The greatest teacher in the world could never win a campaign unless he understood the men he had to lead.—General Omar N. Bradley

And there was a very fitting quote from Hall of Fame Coach Vince Lombardi, who said, "Coaches who can outline plays on a blackboard are a dime a dozen. The ones who win get inside their players and motivate."

Walsh, in his book, also has detailed chapters on the responsibilities of each of his assistants. An example of the duties of an offensive coordinator:

Game analysis: all situations; Scout Report: game plan outline; route sheets. Week: Scripts (scripted plays); Game: play-calling; Location: field; Halftime: coordinates half; list second-half calls; address offense.

By now it should be clear how thorough Walsh was while he was turning a struggling 49er team into a Super Bowl dynasty. In one chapter that focuses on evaluating players, he questions the importance placed on times for the 40-yard dash, calling it "open to question." He uses Hall of Fame receiver Jerry Rice as an example, noting, "Unquestionably, he was the greatest wide receiver in the history of the NFL. Rice's time in the 40-yard dash at the NFL scouting combine was 4.59 seconds. As such, Rice was considered to have marginal speed for a starting wide receiver by virtually every team in the NFL. The only exceptions were the New York Jets, Dallas Cowboys, and the San Francisco 49ers who ultimately drafted him." Walsh said that the 49ers considered his functional speed, rather than his foot speed.

In scouting players, Walsh lists 19 criteria for measuring the skills of a quarterback, including 40-yard fly pattern passes, throwing off sprint action, short curls to a running back, and his functional intelligence evaluation. There are 26 criteria for offensive linemen, including piling on and leading through a hole, a strength test, pass protection against a defender, history of injuries, and experience in playing multiple positions.

The book concludes with 54 pages of schematics, with samples of offensive plays, including Joe Montana's dramatic 12-yard touchdown pass to John Taylor that gave the 49ers a 20–16 win in Super Bowl XXIII. On the play, Rice runs in motion, right-to-left, and breaks outside to attract one of the Bengal safeties. Taylor lines up in a tight end spot, breaks inside Rice, then slants inside and is open for Montana's pass.

Finding the Winning Edge is a comprehensive book on the professional game. A working knowledge of terminology and a feel for organization will help the reader fully appreciate the depths to which Bill Walsh went to become a great coach, but the book is worth reading for anyone pursuing serious play or coaching in the sport.

CHAPTER 20

HOW THE GAME HAS CHANGED

MIAMI AND WASHINGTON once played a Super Bowl in two hours and 29 minutes, culminating in a 14–7 Dolphins win that climaxed an exciting 17-0 perfect season for them. In those early Super Bowl years (That Washington vs. Miami game was Super Bowl VII in Janury 1973), there appeared to be a formula for winning: a solid running game, a smart, high-percentage passer, and a tenacious defense. In that historic Miami win, quarterback Bob Griese threw only 11 passes. Miami's backs—Larry Csonka, Jim Kiick, and Mercury Morris—shared 37 carries and piled up 181 yards, accounting for that very fast game.

The game drew a packed house of 90,192 to the Los Angeles Memorial Coliseum. Still, the NFL owners began feeling that teams were playing too many low-scoring games. Maybe it was a reaction to major league baseball lowering the mound in 1969 to create more offense after the 1968 "Year of the Pitcher." Or to pro basketball speeding up its game. That's when the NFL owners began passing a series of rules designed to create more passing and, therefore, more touchdowns, just like the competing American Football League had done in the '60s to sell tickets.

The AFL had those big arms in Joe Namath, Daryle Lamonica, Babe Parilli, and Len Dawson. But around the NFL, the quarterbacks were known as "field generals" who called their own plays and executed a lot of handoffs, and in those meeting rooms every March, some NFL owners would raise the issue: How can we attract more television viewers and, therefore, bring in more revenue for the teams to share?

To answer that question, the league owners began passing a series of new rules, most of them designed to feature the passing game and turn 16–7 defensive struggles into 34–28 thrillers. Over a short period, the owners eliminated the so-called "bump-and-run technique" that hindered receivers coming out of their breaks. They also eliminated the pass-rusher's head slap. Most importantly, they approved a major rule that allowed pass blockers to extend their arms and jam pass rushers. Under the old pass-blocking rule, blockers had to fold their arms and absorb most of the collision. With the rule change they became the aggressors, and teams began searching for linemen with 38-inch arms and rejecting those with 33-inch arms.

The Pittsburgh Steelers were the first team to embrace the changing offensive rules. At the top of their 1970 draft they took Terry Bradshaw, a strong-armed passer with the deepest drop-back of any quarterback in the league. Four years later, the Steelers drafted Lynn Swann, an acrobatic receiver. Together, they helped the Steelers win four Super Bowls in the '70s, the last two by scores of 35–31 and 31–19. In both of those two games, Bradshaw passed for more than 300 yards. Blended with Franco Harris's weak-side sweeps, Bradshaw's arm gave the Steelers an explosive offense that had the outside effect of bringing more high-profile passers and receivers into the game through the player draft.

The new high-scoring offenses had NFL owners smiling at the growing television ratings and teams wondering where they could find their own big-play passer. In the 1983 draft, there were six quarterbacks taken in the first round; John Elway, Dan Marino, and Jim Kelly became Hall of Famers. Coach Don Shula, who was smart enough to realize that the league was moving towards a pitch-and-catch game, drafted Marino and quickly opened up the Dolphins offense.

Montana at a 49ers practice in 1982, after an agreement was made in response to the 57-day players strike.

Along the way, the best teams began developing their own identities. The Steel Curtain in Pittsburgh, the Hogs' blocking unit in Washington, the Purple People Eaters up in Minnesota, Air Coryell (named after pass-minded coach Don Coryell) in St. Louis and later San Diego), and the Killer-Bs in Miami, where a half-dozen defensive starters had last names beginning with the letter "B."

Then came a 57-day players strike in 1982, in which the union set the table for a system of free agency, minimum salaries, better health plans, and a league-wide salary cap based on league revenues. Meanwhile, game attendance kept increasing, as younger fans flocked to the stadiums to watch quarterbacks wipe out most of the old passing records held by Johnny Unitas, Fran Tarkenton, and Bart Starr. And because of the tricky free agency system and the value of a proven passer, teams began paying huge salaries for their starting quarterbacks—and to fit under the salary cap, the backups had to make a lot less.

Over those changing years, the game evolved into a quarterback-driven league, with teams throwing almost 75 percent of the time. When a team loses its top quarterback, it usually means it also forfeits its chance at reaching the playoffs: Remember Green Bay's Aaron Rodgers with a separated shoulder in 2017? Most of the teams have gone to a three-receiver, one-back offense, virtually eliminating the fullback position, and, if you play tight end, you'd better know how to catch a football, because it's coming to you.

If you need proof that the game has become a pass-and-catch contest, just look at the huge salaries paid to the passers in 2017. Here are the 10 top-rated quarterbacks, listed according to their average per-year salaries:

- Joe Flacco, Baltimore, $22.1 million
- Aaron Rodgers, Green Bay, $22 million
- Russell Wilson, Seattle, $21.9 million
- Ben Roethlisberger, Pittsburgh, $21.85 million
- Eli Manning, New York Giants, $21 million
- Carson Palmer, Arizona, $21 million
- Philip Rivers, Los Angeles Chargers, $20.8 million
- Cam Newton, Carolina, $20.7 million
- Ryan Tannehill, Miami, $19.2 million

And New England's Tom Brady? He's actually ranked seventeenth, with an average salary of $15 million. However, the Patriots gave Brady a $28 million signing bonus in early 2018 and prorated his salary to make it more cap friendly.

Former players' union leader Ed Garvey once proposed that quarterbacks be excluded from the salary cap. The idea made sense, for without having to sacrifice all its other team members' value and talent for the sake of a star quarterback position, teams would have gained stability. The idea never got past the talking stage, and now the league has become a nightmare for teams without a top quarterback.

Unknowingly, perhaps, the NFL owners have turned their game into a league of haves and have-nots. Gone are the years of the run/pass balance, when coaches like New England's Bill Belichick could flood their defenses with specialists, according to the down and distance, on almost every play.

Dan Rooney, the Pittsburgh executive whose Steeler teams always seemed to be ahead of their opponents in sensing trends, warned his fellow owners of selling out to the television networks. "Judgments have to be made about what's good for the game," said Rooney. "That might mean decreasing television revenues. That might mean paying less [in salaries]."

But some of the owners seem to still be digging for higher revenues, meaning more nationally televised games and more television commercials. They have allowed their sport, once a beautifully balanced game of tradition and individual matchups, to morph into a showcase for quarterbacks and acrobatic receivers. There has even been rumors of approving an 18-game schedule with more playoffs, meaning more revenue. Those talks ended when hundreds of former players began filing lawsuits involving concussions they had suffered. As the schedule stands now, we are treated to games on four days or nights each week. Sometimes a one o'clock game, unexpectedly important to the playoffs, can be switched to the same night if the network anticipates a bigger viewing audience.

While salaries continue to rise at all positions (some kickers earn $3 million per year without ever getting their jerseys dirty), the game has drifted towards offense and touchdowns. As former New York Giants general manager George Young once said, "The players are better, but the game isn't as good."

When things don't go right, there is no sign the NFL owners want to restore some balance and flow to their game. Nor does there seem to be a trend with colleges, either, to back away from this pass-crazy game, especially if they recruit a great quarterback.

Indeed, at the 2018 Reese's Senior Bowl, South team coach Bill O'Brien (current Houston Texans coach) had to show one of his quarterbacks how to take a snap from under center. Why? Because that quarterback had operated out of a shotgun set his entire college career.

And remember the old adage, "When you need a tough yard, run your best back over your best blocker." That's not a strategy for Philadelphia Coach Doug Peterson, a former quarterback. He gave the Patriots a play from deep in his playbook, a tight end pass to Nick Foles, his quarterback, for a 1-yard touchdown in 2018's Super Bowl LII. Nobody bothered to cover Foles, because quarterbacks are the sixth eligible receiver on offense and nobody expects them to catch anything—except flak when things don't go right.

CHAPTER 21

VIGNETTES

IN THE SPRING of 1989, Eddie DeBartolo celebrated the 49ers' Super Bowl run of the '80s with a weekend of food, drink, and joy in his hometown of Youngstown, Ohio. It was billed as the "Team of the Eighties" celebration. The 49ers family was housed at the Holiday inn in Boardman, Ohio (built by the DeBartolos), and the three-day affair included dinner at Mr. Anthony's, a five-star restaurant, where guests were treated to a highlight film and served individual filets of beef Wellington and lobster tails, seasonal field greens, bouquetière vegetables and new potatoes, followed by Champignon and fallen chocolate soufflés with a trio of sauces. Music was provided by Jeffrey Osborne, whose band was flown in from California for the celebration. No money changed hands at the Holiday Inn, where room service was available until 3:00 a.m. There was also a special tour of the DeBartolo Corporation facility, and the DeBartolo family also made a $150 contribution to Youngstown area charities in the name of each guest.

***

Former Stanford running back Darrin Nelson recalled his years playing for Bill Walsh. Walsh had a rule against hazing freshmen. He allowed a little teasing and laughter: "Bill met with the entire freshman class of football players to talk about coming to college and being a college person," said Nelson. "One of the things he said was 'Don't worry about your high school girlfriend. She's probably out with your best friend right now.'"

***

The records of head coaches hired in 1976 when Bill Walsh was passed over after retiring Cincinnati Coach Paul Brown failed to give him a recommendation: Buffalo, Jim Ringo, 3–20; Cincinnati, Bill Johnson, 18–15; New York Jets, Lou Holtz, 3–10 (13 games); New Orleans, Hank Stram, 7–21; New York Giants, John McVay, 14–23; Philadelphia, Dick Vermeil, 57–51; San Francisco, Monte Clark, 8–6; Seattle, Jack Patera, 35–59; Tampa Bay, John McKay, 45–91–1.

***

"Bill is a complex man," said offensive tackle Keith Fahnhorst of his head coach. "You have to be some kind of SOB to survive in that business, and a lot of time that's what he is. It's too bad you can't be successful and still be a little bit more human. But maybe you can't be successful if you're too human."

Walsh, about himself, said, "People didn't see me in a social atmosphere, just in the role as head coach of the 49ers, where it can appear that I'm cold and calculating, which is an error. I think I'm a player's coach, but I'm definitely not a good, easy-going, swell guy. Anytime you see a good-old guy, a relaxed and unperturbed steady guy, you're going to have a steady, mediocre team."

***

Before a game against the Pittsburgh Steelers in 1981, Walsh talked to his players about the British troops in Burma as they fought the

Japanese in World War II. The 49ers responded with a grinding 17–14 win in which Carlton Williamson knocked out two Steelers receivers.

"He's always liked war books," said former NFL Coach Dick Vermeil. "I spent a weekend on vacation at his house. His spare bedroom was filled with books about generals and war and strategy. Bill always thought that way. He was, I think, the best," said Vermeil about Walsh's detailing strategy and his ability to inspire toughness and game-day confidence.

Assistant coach Lynn Stiles once said of Walsh's teams, "We practiced fast, quick, and explosive. He was a perfectionist."

Walsh, on his style, said, "We had standards of performance that had to be very high. You have to focus on details, or the players can lose their concentration. We always played with our backs to the wall. Every time we played we were in a survival mode, that nobody could take the game away from us."

***

In their first three Super Bowl years, the 49ers were 20–4 in road games.

***

Walsh sometimes poked fun at his players for a changeup in moods. After he wore a bellhop's outfit and carried Joe Montana's bags before Super Bowl XVI, he dressed as an 1849 prospector attending an awards banquet in Rocklin, California. He wore wire specs and a fake beard, fooling a lot of the guests. Geri, his wife, recalled that he once dressed as the Easter Bunny, saying, "The kids were about two [Craig] and six [Steve]. He was wearing a mask, but it wasn't nearly as successful as that bellhop trick in Detroit. The kids didn't fall for it, not at all."

***

"I saw that white horse on the sideline and the band and the black shoes the players wore, and I said, 'Hey, I gotta do this!'" That's how

Riki Ellison, at his very first football game, reacted after watching Southern Cal play. Born in New Zealand, Ellison had moved to the United States at age eight. He developed into an excellent run-stopping linebacker who earned a scholarship to USC. Despite four knee surgeries, he became the 49ers' fifth-round draft choice in 1983. Said fellow linebacker Jack Reynolds, "Football, dominoes, his train set, Trivial Pursuit. You name it and he's into it," he added. Ellison agreed, saying, "I was jumping off roofs, surfing, playing basketball with my cast on. To be a linebacker, you've got to have something wrong with you. You're playing against guys who outweigh you by 50 pounds. I think I'm a psycho case. I don't hide anything. I just let it all hang loose."

***

Care to take a guess who turned out to be one of the key negotiators when the 49ers were trying to sign sack specialist Fred Dean to a new contract in 1984? That would be California Assembly Speaker and former Sam Francisco Mayor Willie Brown.

"He actually jogged out of our room, then to their room, then back to ours, and so on," said 49ers executive Carmen Policy. "He helped us all maintain a clear mind on viable issues." Said Brown, "I suppose they asked me to do this because I guess politicians do this virtually full-time, trying to break deadlocks between respective sides. Just the dialogue, going back and forth, that was the one key simple factor." Asked what football background he had that helped in the talks, Brown replied, "I have a vast football background. I own six season tickets."

***

Sam Wyche, the 49ers' quarterback coach from 1979 to '82, needed a heart transplant after he retired from coaching. That meant he had to relinquish the pilot's license he had held since 1970. But after he received a new heart, he planned to apply for a new license.

***

Receiver John Taylor makes the winning TD catch with 16 seconds left in Super Bowl XXIII.

John Taylor caught the winning touchdown pass from Joe Montana in Super Bowl XXIII with 16 seconds left to play in one of the game's most exciting finishes. But Taylor remains the forgotten star whenever anybody talks the about 49ers' dynasty. It turns out that Taylor, who caught 347 passes in nine seasons for the 49ers, has almost always been overlooked. After his game-winning catch, a television station near Taylor's home town of Pennsauken, New Jersey, wanted to air some footage of his high school years. "We finally found a clip of him playing defensive back and making a couple of tackles," said Vince McAneney, Taylor's coach.

***

When Bill Walsh got his first look at Pro Bowl guard Randy Cross, he saw him as a future Hall of Famer. "He had a lot of mobility, just a fine all-around athlete," said Walsh. "He could pull on sweeps and was a very good pass protector. And he was a great competitor. You talk about players taking the field when they're injured, he would do it and you wouldn't realize the extent of it until after the game. He was just an inspirational competitor."

***

So, what happened to James Owens, the UCLA running back who was selected one round before Joe Montana in the 1979 draft? The idea was to convert Owens into a receiver. "He had world-class speed," said Walsh. "But he pulled hamstrings every time. One time he took a kickoff and ran it back for a touchdown. Ten yards from the end zone, he fell with another pulled hamstring and limped over the goal line."

***

We will never know if a quarterback named Greg Cook could have played the role of Joe Montana in Cincinnati. Cook was the Bengals' first-round pick in the 1969 draft. He was a prototype passer (6-foot-4, 220 pounds). "He was as good as anybody," said Walsh, who coached Cook with the Bengals. "In his rookie year, he averaged 14 yards an attempt. Every completion was like 25 yards. Whether the defense was man-to-man or a primitive zone, Greg could get the ball there like Dan Marino. The difference he had over Dan was that Greg was a great runner."

Unfortunately, Cook suffered a severe shoulder injury as a rookie in his eleventh game. He tried to come back four years later, but retired after one game. He was claimed by the Kansas City Chiefs in 1975, but never played another down. Years later, he joined seven other quarterbacks, including Joe Montana, Steve DeBerg, Ken Anderson, and Dan

Fouts, in a reunion party for Walsh. Said DeBerg, "Comparing him [Walsh] and other coaches is like comparing a professor at Stanford with a high school teacher."

***

Mike White, who coached briefly for the 49ers in 1978 and '79, remembers the first time he met Bill Walsh, who was to become one of his closest friends: "I went to high school with his wife, Geri," said White. "I think I met Bill in 1960, when I was at Cal [Cal-Berkeley]. He comes in, and he had written his thesis on defensive football. You know Bill. This was a 500-page thesis on defensive football. That's how our relationship started."

***

Eason Ramson was a backup tight end for the 49ers who struggled with a drug problem that eventually sent him to prison. "When I was in prison, my mother passed away," he recalled. "My sister called Bill [Walsh] and said, 'Coach ....'and Bill said, 'No, I'm more than a coach. I'm a friend.' He offered financial help," Ramson recalled, "and then he came to visit me in prison." Ramson feared a long prison term, but Walsh intervened. "I was facing 'three strikes' when Bill wrote to the judge and said I was worth saving." Ramson got out of prison and began a new life helping troubled kids.

***

Eddie DeBartolo on Walsh: "He is, without hesitation, the greatest coach who has ever coached this game,"

***

John McVay on 49ers salaries: "We didn't have the NFL's highest-paid starters. Ronnie Lott was the only guy we had who led the league in salary at his position. But we did have the league's highest-paid backups."

***

Dwight Clark on the coaches' confidence: "You could hear the confidence in the way they were talking. The closer the game got, instead of getting more uptight, Bill [Walsh] and Sam [Wyche] and all the other coaches seemed to get more confident and more loose about the game. Like they knew we were better, they knew we should win."

***

Bill Walsh called his 1984 team "The greatest football team and the greatest group of people I've had the pleasure of being associated with during my coaching career. Without doubt, this is the best team in pro football today." That team finished with a 15–1 record and won Super Bowl XIX. Then, four years later, Walsh said his 1988 team that finished 13–6 and won Super Bowl XXIII was the best in the history of pro football. The thought behind Walsh's reevaluation was that he didn't want to leave receiver Jerry Rice, drafted in 1985, off his "best team."

***

Joe Montana's performances in winning four Super Bowls produced these remarkable statistics: 83 completions in 122 attempt Bowls; 11 touchdowns; and not a single interception.

***

In the seasons in which the 49ers didn't win a Super Bowl, Bill Walsh thought most of the criticism came from Eddie DeBartolo's Youngstown friends. "There was pressure on Eddie," Walsh said. "It was from his Youngstown friends. 'How can you have this kind of team? How can you lose? How did that guy drop that pass?' At some point they say, 'It's got to be your coach.' But Eddie held them off. But there isn't any question, it came from those people in Youngstown. I don't think it came from Eddie DeBartolo, Sr. But no, he was under that kind of pressure from his friends."

***

Bill Walsh thought that the 49ers' 28–3 romp over the Bears in the 1988 NFC title game in Chicago's bone-chilling weather was the best game one of his teams ever played. "It was amazing," he said. "Our defense just stopped them. They were 14–2 and were very positive about beating us. They were called the 'Team of Destiny.'"

***

Former Stanford Athletic Director Ted Leland recalled how Bill Walsh had angered University of Washington fans by criticizing the school's football team before their game. "When Bill got off the plane in Seattle, all of the press were waiting," recalled Leland. "He put on one of those fake noses and glasses. It diffused the whole thing. Even they had to laugh."

***

Roy Lott, father of Hall of Famer Ronnie Lott, was his son's presenter in 2000. "Ronnie set an example by obtaining his degree [from Southern California] in four years," he said. "A leader of his family, encouraging his children to become beneficial members of society, a leader in his community, he developed an organization to help all children to have a better chance at life. All-Stars Helping Kids sponsors many educational and health projects. These projects let children know that their hopes and their dreams are only a step away. Ronnie, through his spirit of giving, leading, and love has made the world a better place for all people, especially for those who have had the chance to have a friendship with the man behind the helmet."

***

WHEN THE 49ERS WERE KINGS

The 49ers ended their first season under new coach Kyle Shanahan with 18 players on injured reserve. The hardest hit unit was defense, with 12 players down, including six from the secondary.

***

When he looks back on the 49ers' dynasty years, Eddie DeBartolo remembers mostly the closeness of the players and the organization. "Bill Walsh and the whole organization and the closeness to the players," he said, "that's what I remember. "All those years of playing together, that's what made it. It was so special."

***

In Super Bowl XXIII, his final game, Bill Walsh said the 49ers had to stay with their base defense because of Cincinnati's no-huddle offense. "We didn't substitute like we normally would to avoid the no-huddle problem," he said. "Sam [Wyche] was notorious for getting caught with 12 men on the field, and he's going to get a five-yard penalty. You'd like to have your nickel [five defensive backs] out there, but you went with your regular guys against whatever they had."

***

Bill Walsh on receiver Jerry Rice: "His conditioning was excellent. He was strong, too. He wasn't stronger from the standpoint of muscle development, but you couldn't knock him off-stride very well. If you bounced into him, he would win the contest. Above and beyond that, he had beautiful hands and was very, very intelligent about thinking on every pass route he ran. And he had nerve, a lot of nerve to go for the football."

***

Cincinnati Coach Sam Wyche was mic'd for Super Bowl XXIII, which Bill Walsh learned when he watched the highlight film. "He was walking up and down the sideline, talking to his players," said Walsh. "He's saying, 'They're going to throw to Rice . . . . They're going to throw to Rice," just before our winning touchdown pass." Jerry Rice, however, turned out to be a decoy, as Joe Montana threw the winning touchdown pass to John Taylor.

ACKNOWLEDGMENTS

I WOULD FIRST LIKE to thank Skyhorse Publishing for its interest in a book on the dynasty years of the San Francisco 49ers. There have been a number of previous books on Coach Bill Walsh, quarterback Joe Montana, receiver Jerry Rice, and other 49ers. I decided to take a different approach. I linked the 49ers' success to the return of hope and promise in their beloved city after two tragic murders.

I am indebted to authors Mike Silver, Glenn Dickey, Scott Ostler, Bob Oates, and Lowell Cohn for providing me with background material on the 49ers' dynasty years. I also want to thank Karen and Glenn Donohue for steering me through the jungle of the internet, executive assistants Amy Swander and Ty Hawkins for their help in arranging my interviews with Eddie DeBartolo Jr., and Mona Valore for offering suggestions on this project.

Owner Eddie DeBartolo Jr. was kind to give me his time in a very busy schedule. Amy Swander and Ty Hawkins, his executive assistants, set up my interviews. The 49ers staff and coaches were extremely helpful. Aside from the two main characters upon which this book is based, I would like to cite executive John McVay and coaches Sam Wyche and Bill McPherson. The 49ers were a unique team. The football operation was as close to a family of coaches, players, and staffers as you could possibly imagine. Indeed, the team took its framework and affection from the DeBartolo Construction Company in Youngstown, Ohio. What other team in NFL history has had a coach call his players to say, simply, "I love you."

Bill Walsh was the most remarkable person I have ever met. I was lucky. I spent nearly a week with this legendary coach who never complained about his fatal blood disease. His team is now under a different owner and plays for a new, imaginative coach, Kyle Shanahan. Perhaps they can win another Super Bowl for this great city of hopes and dreams.

SOURCES

Thanks to:
49ers 2007 media guide
49ers alumni newsletter
Kansas City Chiefs press packet
San Francisco Chronicle
Sports Illustrated (coverage by Mike Silver)
Los Angeles Times
Philadelphia Daily News
Ray Didinger
Personal interviews
– Bill Walsh
– Sam Wyche
– Ed DeBartolo Jr.; DeBartolo website; DeBartolo Hall of Fame speech
– Tom Benson
– Jim Miller
– Deion Sanders
– Carmen Policy
– John McVay
– Brian Billick
– Steven Kay

- — Dave Schinski
- — Keith Fahnhorst

NFL Draft Encyclopedia

Go Long: The Journey Beyond the Game and Fame, by Jerry Rice with Brian Curtis

Secrets of an NFL Scout, by Tony Razzano with Richard Weiner

Finding the Winning Edge, by Bill Walsh with Brian Billick and James Peterson

The Making of the Super Bowl, by Don Weiss

Fodor's San Francisco